IMPROVING
STUDENT
LEARNING
WHEN BUDGETS ARE
TIGHT

IMPROVING
STUDENT
LEARNING
WHEN BUDGETS ARE
TIGHT

ALLAN R. ODDEN

CORWIN
A SAGE Company

CORWIN
A SAGE Company

FOR INFORMATION:

Corwin

A SAGE Company

2455 Teller Road

Thousand Oaks, California 91320

(800) 233-9936

Fax: (800) 417-2466

www.corwin.com

SAGE Ltd.

1 Oliver's Yard

55 City Road

London, EC1Y 1SP

United Kingdom

SAGE India Pvt. Ltd.

B 1/I 1 Mohan Cooperative Industrial Area

Mathura Road, New Delhi

India 110 044

SAGE Asia-Pacific Pte. Ltd.

33 Pekin Street #02-01

Far East Square

Singapore 048763

Acquisitions Editor: Debra Stollenwerk

Associate Editor: Desirée A. Bartlett

Editorial Assistant: Kimberly Greenberg

Production Editor: Cassandra Margaret Seibel

Copy Editor: Erin Livingston

Typesetter: Hurix Systems (P) Ltd.

Proofreader: Wendy Jo Dymond

Indexer: Terri Corry

Cover Designer: Rose Storey

Permissions Editor: Adele Hutchinson

Printed in the United States of America.

Library of Congress Cataloging-in-Publication Data

Odden, Allan.

Improving student learning when budgets are tight / Allan R. Odden.

p. cm.

Includes bibliographical references and index.

ISBN 978-1-4522-1708-6 (pbk.)

1. School improvement programs—United States. 2. School budgets—United States. I. Title.

LB2822.82.O33 2012

371.2'07—dc23

2011045908

This book is printed on acid-free paper.

MIX
Paper from responsible sources
FSC
www.fsc.org
FSC® C014174

12 13 14 15 16 10 9 8 7 6 5 4 3 2 1

Contents

List of Tables

Preface

Purpose

In these times, when money for education is very tight and many states and districts are cutting education budgets, the links between the resource side of education reform and school improvement have become one of the most critical issues for sustaining our nation's schools. Without a more effective use of the education dollar, current fiscal constraints and funding cuts could lead to battles over money, ineffective across-the-board budget cuts, and a lower-quality education system, all with a negative impact on student learning.

This book is intended to show pathways through this current fiscal mess by linking what is known about improving schools and student performance to more effective and efficient resource-use practices. This is not a conceptual book about what possibly could be done in a hypothesized future, such as giving all parents vouchers to choose the school they want their children to attend, eliminating collective bargaining so teacher compensation can be cut, or shifting to contract public schools. This book is about concrete, specific actions that can be taken now, without major changes in the organization and governance of America's school systems. Debates about these long-term changes in the American education system should occur, but state, district, and school leaders and all teachers need ideas and strategies they can implement now, not in some ideal or newly conceptualized future. The proposed changes represent tough decisions for school leaders and will be not be sustained unless school leaders are given political support by school boards, the public, political leaders outside of education, and teacher unions.

To weather current fiscal storms, effective resource-use practices must be connected to the overall education improvement (or, in some cases, turnaround strategy), the budget that exists (state and district leaders must deal with the budget they have, not the budget they'd like to have), and the talent needed to execute the improvement or turnaround strategy. Put differently, to boost student performance, each district and school needs an improvement strategy, resource allocation and use practices that undergird that strategy, and the teacher, principal, and central office talent needed to implement the strategy. All three are important and all three will be addressed here. In fact, this book is the only one in the country that addresses all three issues (as well as others) in comprehensive, coherent, and specific ways. The book also suggests that the time has arrived to tap the power of technology, as nearly all K–12 school programs today can be accessed online.

Audience

The audience for this book includes teachers, principals and other education administrators, school boards, teacher unions, local political leaders, and state policymakers—in short, everyone now struggling with how to confront the severe revenue shortages in the public sector while maintaining the momentum for education reform and continuing to improve student achievement and close achievement gaps. The book is anchored in a *Plan of Action*, which discusses how schools can improve and includes multiple, specific ideas for better resource use that will be of high interest to educators in schools making micro-decisions on school organization and resource allocation as well as education leaders at the district and state levels who are making macro-decisions about school budgeting and human capital management strategies. In several chapters, the book identifies how these local actions can be reinforced or structured by state policies and regulations. Thus, the book will be of interest to schools and districts as well as state education and political leaders. As such, the book also could function as a supplement in education administration courses, including school improvement, the principalship, education budgeting, and school finance.

Organization

The book begins with an overview chapter on what is known about improving and turning around schools and student performance, while subsequent chapters address specific issues—such as resources, strategic budgeting, educator talent, and technology—related to those specific improvement strategies. The book does not simply address ways to reduce budgets or do things more efficiently but also relates all recommendations back to the Plan of Action developed in the first chapter. The book has a separate chapter on issues relating to teacher and principal talent, including a section on new approaches to teacher compensation and a section on teacher pensions; the latter suggests a better and more economically efficient way to structure teacher pensions that does not just shift the entire burden of having a pension onto the backs of educators. The book concludes with a separate chapter that addresses how to set priorities for situations that require budget cuts, which is the situation for many districts and schools around the country. Thus, although the book stresses changes that can be made in the use of fiscal resources in the short term, it also addresses some long-term issues such as teacher salary structures and pensions and the potential for more use of technology in providing educational services.

1. A Plan of Action: Turning Around Low-Performing and Enhancing High-Performing Schools

Chapter 1 draws from my own research (Odden, 2009; Odden & Archibald, 2009) as well as ongoing research by others (e.g., Blankstein, 2010; Chenoweth, 2007; Miles & Frank, 2008) on what it takes to dramatically improve student performance and reduce the achievement gaps that plague too many school systems. It identifies 12 strategies that have emerged from a wide range of literature, including the turnaround literature from the last few years. The strategies discussed include the following:

- analyzing initial data to understand the current performance context (i.e., creating a sense of urgency for retaining the focus on boosting student performance even in tough fiscal times)
- setting specific, numeric, and high goals and using those goals to drive resource allocation priorities
- selecting a curriculum program and developing a view of effective instruction practice, with more specific comments on the characteristics of effective reading programs
- understanding the trade-offs between core subjects (reading/ English/language arts, mathematics, science, history, and foreign language) and electives, the use of time and school schedules, and the emergence of career-technical programs to replace the old vocational education programs
- developing formative and benchmark assessments and using data to improve instructional practice
- organizing teacher work into collaborative teams

- completing ongoing, comprehensive professional development, which includes the use of instructional coaches
- developing strategies for struggling students including Tier 1, 2, and 3 strategies in the Response to Intervention approach to students who need extra help
- utilizing leadership
- using teacher, principal, and central office talent

2. The Resource Needs of the Plan of Action

Chapter 2 addresses in very specific terms the resource needs and costs of each of the strategies discussed in Chapter 1. It ends with a brief description of how the full resource needs of all the strategies discussed in Chapter 1 can be linked to state school-funding formulas to determine one way of calculating an adequate level of education spending (Odden & Picus, 2008; Odden, Picus, & Goetz 2010). By making this link, the chapter links the micro-issues of effective resource needs to the macro-issues of state school finance policy. Each of the major resource recommendations includes a citation to a randomized control trial that finds the individual strategy to positively impact student achievement and to a randomized control trail that finds all of these recommendations together to boost student learning.

3. Targeting Resources to Student Learning When Budgets Are Tight

This chapter discusses multiple possibilities both for cutting back budgets in strategic ways and for targeting resources to the all the elements of the Plan of Action—regardless of the budget context. It first discusses the cost increase pressures that bear down on schools and consume budget dollars in good and bad fiscal times. It then shows how districts and schools that have more than the resources described in Chapter 2 could cut back to the levels recommended in that chapter, with the argument being that such cuts would have little or no impact on student learning. Then Chapter 3 discusses how schools and districts can be nimble and strategic about using the resources they have. Chapter 3 identifies flexibilities schools actually have in setting class sizes and multiple variations of class size that reflect efficient use of resources as well as support high levels of student achievement, including the costs (and savings) of lowering/raising class sizes by one to three students. It discusses the cost elements of school schedules; the differential costs associated with having six-, seven-, and eight-period days; and the links among cost, school schedules, and teacher individual plan time and collaborative team time. It discusses how and why some districts spend significantly more on electives than core courses (Roza, 2010), and the modest costs of emerging high-quality career-technical programs such as Project Lead the Way. It addresses the costs of formative (or *short cycle*) and benchmark assessments, and the specific costs of various ways to structure Tier 2 interventions such as tutoring in groups of one to five students and extended-day and summer school programs. It identifies research that shows that if high-quality core instruction is provided to all students (Tier 1), followed by effective Tier 2 strategies, then the incidents of students needing special education services can drop by 50 percent, thus reducing the costs of special education.

4. Recruiting, Developing, and Compensating Top Educator Talent: Local Practices and Supporting State Policies

Chapter 4 addresses educator talent. It includes three focused sections: one on recruiting and retaining educator talent, a second on revising teacher salary structures, and a third on revising educator pensions (both their structure and who pays for them).

The talent section summarizes new approaches for how schools and districts can acquire the teacher, principal, and central office talent needed to implement rigorous, comprehensive, robust, and effective educational improvement strategies. Drawing from my new book that analyzes these issues in more depth (Odden, 2011a), the chapter then addresses teacher and principal talent acquisition, motivation and development, evaluation, and retention and their key state policy implications. This section also discusses the costs of partnering with new talent organizations such as Teach For America and The New Teacher Project to recruit better teacher talent, the costs of professional development issues related to new and more comprehensive ways to evaluate teachers (and the core costs of these approaches), and the specifics of the cost aspects of cutting staff by effectiveness rather than seniority.

The next section addresses teacher compensation and the appropriate state role in stimulating new strategic directions in redesigning teacher salary schedules. It links the measures of effectiveness discussed in the first section of this chapter to new ways to pay teachers for knowledge and skills (rather than experience and education), for teaching in content areas experiencing teacher shortages, and for teaching in high-poverty/low-performing schools. The chapter also discusses the costs of these new approaches to teacher pay as well as the sources of funding districts can use to fund these new compensation strategies, arguing that the prime source for funding new approaches to teacher compensation is the current salary budget.

Finally, the last section of this chapter discusses educator pensions and the emerging literature on their costs and unequal benefits in the context of pressures across the country to rein in pension costs and make them more equitable as well as more predictable for teachers, principals, and other educators. Defined benefit public pensions are under attack both because they provide more predictable pensions than do 401(k)-type defined contribution plans and because many are underfunded (though mainly because states have not appropriated their share each year). It discusses the issue of educators artificially inflating their final average year salaries (thus increasing their pension payouts) and shows how public pensions primarily reward employees who stay in one education system for their entire work life and shortchange those who are more mobile, which is more characteristic of workers today. Though the prime policy shift across the country is to drop defined benefit programs and replace them with 401(k)-type pension programs, which shifts the responsibility for pensions from the public to the individual, an emerging hybrid approach—the cash balance pension—controls costs, links pension payouts to earnings over the lifetime of an individual, and balances individual and organization (the government, in the case of educators) responsibility for pensions. This section reviews all these issues and recommends that states move to the cash balance approach, which seems to be the fairest, most affordable, and most economically sound new approach to providing individuals with pensions.

5. Computers and Technology in Education: Costs and Online Options

Chapter 5 provides an overview of the various online learning options that have evolved and are being used in the K–12 education system. The first part of the chapter specifies the costs of equipping schools with sufficient computer technologies so that, if desired, curriculum and instructional delivery can fully tap the power of computer technologies. The second part of the chapter describes the accelerating use of online programs to deliver education services and then describes the key features and costs of three major categories of online educational programming: state virtual schools, private sector programs such as K12 Inc. and Connections Academy, and "blended instruction," which is a combination of brick-and-mortar schooling and online programming. This part of the chapter notes that most Advanced Placement (AP) programs are now available online at modest cost. The chapter argues that the Internet and computer technologies that exist today already offer ways to educate many (though not all) students that are both as effective as a regular classroom and cost much less, and suggests that in these tight fiscal times states, districts, and schools should seriously consider incorporating these technological possibilities into their curriculum and instructional strategies.

6. When Budget Cuts Are Necessary

The last chapter is a summary, bringing all the strategies discussed in the book together to address the issues of what to do if, after resource reallocation, restructuring school programs, and implementing every possible efficiency, budget cuts are still needed. Issues addressed include (a) salary freezes as opposed to salary schedule freezes, (b) increasing employee contributions to health and pension benefits, (c) increasing class size by modest amounts, (d) changing school schedules from seven- and eight-period days to six-period days, (e) dismissing educators based on effectiveness rather than on seniority, and so on. The chapter describes how these changes can be made for a handsomely funded elementary school, a low-funded high school, and a modestly funded middle school, as examples of how different schools can engage in the strategic budgeting process even when dollars must be cut. The goal of this chapter is to show how budget cuts can be made without negatively impacting the core instructional program and while retaining fairness between public sector costs and educator salaries and benefits when there is a broader economic slowdown, simultaneously possibly improving both the effectiveness and efficiency of the education dollar.

In short, the book is a guide for principals and education system leaders through the fiscal thicket they face for the next several years. It offers detailed guidance for how to link strategies that will boost student learning to budget practices, how budget cuts can be made while retaining a powerful instructional improvement program, and where new dollars could be invested in strategic ways. The book also identifies the current financial pressures that the public places on schools, which erodes the fiscal ability of school leaders to implement the strategies outlined in the book, and argues in many places for broader political and public support for the tough decisions detailed in the book, because educators cannot make the tough—but necessary—budget decisions required unless the political community supports them.

Acknowledgments

I would like to thank my administrative assistant, Lisa Armstrong, for tracking down all the references for this book; she is tops at this task. I also would like to thank my research assistant, Alan Nathan, a PhD student in the School of Education's Department of Educational Leadership and Policy Analysis, for his research on how schools are currently using technology to provide more and more services online. I am also indebted to the many, many teachers, principals, and central office leaders who created many of the strategies discussed in the book and had the courage to implement them in their schools and districts; their students have benefited from these more-effective uses of the education dollar.

Publisher's Acknowledgments

In addition, Corwin would like to thank the following individuals for taking the time to provide their editorial insight and guidance:

Kenneth Arndt, Superintendent
Community Unit School District 300
Carpentersville, IL

Judy Brunner, Author, Consultant, Clinical Faculty
Missouri State University, Instructional Solutions Group
Springfield, MO

Margarete Couture, Elementary Principal
South Seneca Central School District
Interlaken, NY

Peter Dillon, Superintendent of Schools
Berkshire Hills Regional School District
Stockbridge, MA

Douglas Hesbol, District Administrator
Laraway Community Consolidated School District 70C
Joliet, IL

Mary Johnstone, Principal
Rabbit Creek Elementary School
Anchorage, AK

Neil MacNeill, Headmaster
Ellenbrook Primary School
Ellenbrook, Western Australia

About the Author

 **Allan R. Odden** is Professor of Educational Leadership and Policy Analysis at the University of Wisconsin–Madison; he also is codirector of the Consortium for Policy Research in Education (CPRE) and Director of Strategic Management of Human Capital (SMHC), a CPRE Project focused on talent and human capital management in education. He formerly was Professor of Education Policy and Administration at the University of Southern California (1984–1993), and Assistant Executive Director of the Education Commission of the States (1975–1984). He also was a mathematics teacher and curriculum developer at Benjamin Franklin High School in New York City's East Harlem (1967–1972). He earned his PhD from Teachers College, Columbia University in 1975. He is an international expert on effective resource use in education, the strategic management of human capital in education, teacher performance-based compensation, teacher performance evaluations, education finance, resource allocation and use, resource reallocation, school-based management, and educational policy development and implementation. He directed several federal-funded and foundation-funded research centers from 1990 to 2009. He has worked with scores of districts on education fiscal issues and talent management issues and has advised state education and political leaders in more than 35 states and several countries, always seeking to translate research into the best practices, supported by effective policies. He has published over 250 journal articles and book chapters and 35 books. In many ways, *Improving Student Learning When Budgets Are Tight* is a culmination of his research career, which has focused on improving student performance by linking school improvement efforts to local budget practices and state school finance systems.

1

A Plan of Action

Turning Around Low-Performing and Enhancing High-Performing Schools

- Garden Grove (CA), Long Beach (CA), Aldine (TX), and Boston (MA) have all doubled student performance in reading or math over a four- to six-year period during the past decade. A central element of their improvement plans was a systemic view of effective instructional practices.

- Rosalia (WA), a small, rural district in Washington with high concentrations of students from non-English-speaking backgrounds, and Abbotsford (WI), a similar district in rural Wisconsin that experienced a large influx of students born in Mexico, doubled student performance in reading even as the demographics of their student body changed.

- Madison (WI), Richmond (VA), and several other urban districts have dramatically increased student performance in reading by implementing a structured reading program across the district, supported by ongoing professional development, instructional coaches in reading, and one-to-one tutoring for struggling students.

The fact is that scores of districts and schools across the country in all kinds of communities have produced large, measurable gains in student performance in reading and mathematics by using extant dollars more effectively. The issue is whether these success stories can be expanded even during these times of tight and falling budgets. The book shows how such success stories can continue.

The fiscal context for education has changed. Whether called a new fiscal normal or the new era of austerity, the fact is that the twentieth-century pattern of continued rise in education revenues and resultant education spending is over. The fiscal crisis of 2008–2011 is shining a fiscal accountability light on public schools, and neither political leaders nor the public are happy. Fairly or unfairly, more and more people point to rising school spending and continued flat—or only modestly rising—student achievement and ask, "Why?"

In early 2011, the fiscal side of school reform created two new pressures on schools. The first pressure was the likelihood that the stimulus funds that had blunted funding cuts for the previous two years were spent and would not be replaced by state (or local) dollars, thus presenting school districts with significant new funding cuts, called *the funding cliff*. The second pressure involved the claims that, in general, public sector salary and benefits—more specifically those for educators—were too generous. Though the bulk of workers in the private sector had experienced various combinations of salary freezes, salary cuts, and increased contributions to benefits—to wit, compensation cuts—most public sector workers, including most educators, had experienced few of those realities. In fact, too many educators and their organizational leaders up to that time had refused to even consider a salary freeze, let alone paying more for benefits.

Regardless of one's view on these various issues, the fact is that school budgets will be tight for several years—if not decades—to come. Compounding the above issues are two related facts: First, the public and most political leaders seem to be unwilling to raise taxes to continue expanding public services; second, demands for other services such as health care, programs for senior citizens, support for increasing numbers of persons in poverty, and other public commitments (including prisons) mean tight state and local budgets are pressured by multiple noneducational issues as well.

The bottom line is that revenues for schools, which has tracked higher and higher every decade for the past 50 years, are unlikely to continue that pattern. A rosy prediction would be for education revenues to keep pace with inflation; a more reasonable scenario would be level education funding (which has no increase in absolute dollars); the actual reality might be a decline in dollars per pupil—not just real (i.e., inflation-adjusted) numbers but actual dollar-per-pupil declines. Indeed, Texas, which in early 2011 was growing by 60,000 students each year, cut state aid in absolute terms by hundreds of millions of dollars for the next biennium; California had to both cut education funding and raise taxes to keep cuts to a minimum, and the bulk of other states simply had less in both state and local coffers, which made it difficult—if not impossible—to keep the education budget "harmless." Indeed, the June 2011 report of the Center on Education Policy found that 70 percent of school districts across the country had budget cuts in 2010–2011, and 60 percent said they had to cut in 2011–2012 as well. Most said that such cuts were hampering progress on school reform (Center on Education Policy, 2011).

Compounding these pessimistic fiscal realities are continuing pressures to increase student performance and close achievement gaps. Indeed, as more and more educators, policymakers, and leaders recognize the demographics of schooling (falling percentages of middle-income children and rising percentages of poverty-impacted children), the resulting stagnation—if not decline—in student achievement, and the knowledge demands of the brain-based global economy, the need to boost student achievement becomes not just an equity imperative but an economic imperative as well. Simply put, despite falling school budgets, educators must boost student learning. Falling education budgets cannot slow education reform; change must continue regardless of the budget situation.

Thus, though the initial responses to the fiscal crisis that started in 2008 and shook the country in 2009 were modest (with most states, districts, and schools continuing with business as usual and administering nonstrategic budget cutbacks), the educational fiscal game needs to change in the future. Schools can't continue to cut programs without changes in compensation levels for educators. Districts can't continue to cut across the board—fewer counselors, no librarians, less art and music, and higher class sizes—with no plan for moving forward. States can't continue to cut aid and maintain the rules and regulations for all categorical programs, especially with weak accountability systems for student learning.

States, districts, and schools must figure out how to set new strategic directions and align their dollars with programs, strategies, and systems that together boost student learning, whether the overall budget stays the same or must be reduced. The new era of fiscal austerity for public schools will require educators to rethink all aspects of the education system—how it recruits, compensates, and retains top teacher and educator talent; how it organizes curriculum and instructional services; how it uses technology to boost productivity (without simply raising costs); how it embraces accountability for student results; and most importantly, how it uses the education dollar more effectively and efficiently, regardless of the size of the education budget.

A Strategic Approach to Using the Education Dollar

Using the education dollar strategically is not accomplished simply by cutting budgets or increasing class sizes because it saves or frees up money or having educators pay more for their benefits while possibly taking a salary freeze or cut. Using the education dollar strategically is also not accomplished simply by decentralizing decisions about spending to schools or changing the governance of the education system. Using the education dollar strategically is not accomplished by saying that the dollars will be used only for programs and services that benefit the students, as that rationale has been used almost universally for decades.

A strategic approach to using the education dollar means aligning the use of resources to a solid, powerful, and comprehensive education-improvement strategy—a specific and delineated Plan of Action designed to boost student learning and proved as effective in doing so. For low-performing schools, this could be a turnaround strategy. For average-performing schools, this would be a strategy to move them from good to great. And for high-performing schools—of which there are too few in the United States—this would be a strategy to boost performance to world-class standards as well as to have high-performance levels exist for students from low-income backgrounds as well as minority backgrounds. Further, using the education dollar strategically would mean specific and clear links between the resource and staffing needs of the improvement strategy and the allocation of the dollars toward those resources and staffing needs.

Chapters 1 and 2 show how these resources specifications and dollar links can be accomplished. The remainder of Chapter 1 outlines a Plan of Action that has been used by scores of schools and districts across the country to successfully boost student achievement by large increments; Chapter 2 identifies the resource needs of these strategies. Much of the remainder of the book, then, anchors recommendations for changes in the use of resources—whether via resource reallocation or budget cuts—to the prescriptions for resource use that flow from these first two chapters. Put differently, this book begins with a discussion of what needs to be done to dramatically improve student learning and has these strategies and their resource needs drive most other suggestions in the book for more strategic fiscal use practices. In addition, however, the book also addresses the need to be smarter and more strategic about the

85 percent of funds spent on staff—dollars that are almost spent unconsciously. The book also points to how technology can be tapped to boost student performance. But the bulk of the book rests on the powerful education improvement strategy—Plan of Action—described here.

A Plan of Action for Dramatically Improving Student Performance

The main outlines of a comprehensive strategy to improve student learning and close the achievement gaps in schools with diverse student populations are not a secret. They have been described in countless case studies, books, articles, and now publications from school turnaround centers that have emerged during President Obama's and Secretary of Education Arne Duncan's administrations (Blankstein, 2010; Chenoweth, 2007; Education Trust, 2009; Fullan, 2010; Mass Insight Education, 2011; Odden, 2009; Odden & Archibald, 2009). The strategy includes about a dozen key elements[1]:

1. analyzing the current performance situation

2. setting high goals

3. changing curriculum and defining effective instructional practices

4. being strategic about core versus elective courses

5. using data to improve instruction

6. organizing teachers into collaborative groups

7. investing in ongoing, comprehensive, and intensive professional development

8. implementing linked and tiered strategies to help struggling students meet rigorous performance standards

9. distributing leadership across all levels and all roles

10. creating a professional culture

11. taking the acquisition, development, and retention of teacher and principal talent absolutely seriously

12. embracing a culture of accountability for student achievement results

Analyzing the Current Performance Situation

At some point, all districts and school that have dramatically improved student performance take stock of their current student performance situation. Often this is the first step. It is hard to craft a strategy to improve performance if little is known about the level and characteristics of a school's or district's existing student performance. Most schools engage in this process by analyzing the results of state tests, many of which now include not only reading and mathematics but also writing and science, and increasingly analyzing high school end-of-course exams in subjects such as Algebra 1, Algebra 2 (the minimum math level for most career technical programs), biology, and chemistry. The student performance data are analyzed for overall patterns—the percentage of students scoring at or above a proficiency or passing level, the percentage of students scoring at or above the advanced level, and so on; how the results vary by grade level and subject and within subject by type of question—fact and knowledge versus application and problem solving; and how the results vary by student characteristics—all students, students from lower-income backgrounds, students learning English, students with disabilities, and majority versus minority students.

In the most successful cases, these analyzes are conducted by teachers and administrators in each school; through this analytic process, they come to know the performance situation of their students in their school. Increasingly, districts and states have facilitated access to and analyses of this student performance data—the more the actual analytic process can be driven by and involve all faculty, the more the results permeate the school and its culture and the more the faculty will take ownership of the analytic results.

Most faculty data reviews produce surprises during this analytic process. One district discovered that the overall percentage of 60 percent of students scoring at or above grade level was composed of a much higher level of performance for white and a much lower level of performance for minority students—an inequity that was professionally embarrassing and that was discovered only by disaggregating the data by student characteristics. Other schools with very low overall performance levels discovered just how low those levels were, and when below something like 15 percent of students were discovered to have scored at or above proficiency, this produced a resolve to do much, much better. In one urban district, the results showed that performance was slowly rising overall for all subgroups when just analyzing the percentage scoring at proficient levels or above, but when the percentage at advanced levels was analyzed, it showed that large and rising percentages of whites were performing at the advanced level, but that very small and stagnant percentages of African American students performed at the advanced level. This racial achievement gap had been missed until a new analysis (which analyzed both performance indicators) was conducted as part of a process to create a strategic plan.

During the process of analyzing the existing performance situation, few if any of the dramatically improving schools and districts complained about the state test. Most knew it was not perfect; most wished for more performance-oriented and problem-solving questions. But none disputed the overall findings, especially when they showed low performance levels, gaps between various groups of students, or modest improvements during the past several years. Most concluded that change was needed, that their students needed to do better, that they had it within their power to produce those changes, and that a "better" state test would not change the results and might even show the situation as worse.

Few places analyzed just student demographics; after all, schools cannot change the demographics of their students. They are what they are. What can be changed are curriculum and instructional practices that positively impact the students that attend the school. The noted anomaly here (Childress, Doyle, & Thomas, 2009) was Montgomery County, an affluent county in Maryland that borders our nation's capital. The then-new superintendent, Jerry Weast, led the district in a demographic analysis to show that the district's student characteristics were changing and that, if resource allocation and instructional practices did not change, the county would lose its reputation as a high-performing district. The analysis spurred multiple changes, including a macro-shift of resources toward schools with rising percentages of economically disadvantaged students. In short, the district responded positively to its demographic challenges, and Montgomery County now remains one of the highest-performing large districts in the country, including high performance of its low income and African American students. As one specific example, the district produces more minority students who take and pass Advanced Placement (AP) exams than any district in the country, and it is far from the largest district, so this accomplishment results from its educational initiatives and changes in the allocation of resources.

Analyzing student performance data requires few resources. It does require time for teachers and administrators to engage in the analysis, but as argued below, if the district or school has a comprehensive and ongoing professional development program, there will be time for such performance analyses.

Setting High Goals

After analyzing the current performance situation, districts and schools that make dramatic improvement—sometimes literally doubling student performance on state tests—set very high and ambitious goals. They want to be the best urban district in the country. They want to be the best high school in the state. One such large, urban high school had a reputation for being one of the top high schools for African American students; a new principals said, "Why just [be] a good high school for minority students? Why don't we become one of the best high schools in the state (despite our demographics)?" And it did.

Others set eye-popping goals, such as doubling the number of students taking and passing AP classes (Long Beach, CA), doubling the number of minority students achieving at the advanced levels, or increasing the percentage of students performing at least at grade level to 90+ percent, regardless again of the demographics of the school.

Other goals are specific, numeric, and subject focused: increasing the percentage of students scoring at or above proficiency in reading from 55 to 90 percent, increasing the percentage scoring at the advanced level in mathematics from 25 to 50 percent, increasing the percentage of students passing Algebra 1 within three semesters from 50 to 75 percent, and so on.

I have studied schools and districts with less ambitious improvement goals, such as simply to improve student performance in reading and mathematics or to have a net of one student in the school improve his or her performance level—and those schools and districts made equally modest, underwhelming improvements.

It should be clear that these kind of ambitious, eye-popping goals are not just "stretch goals" that the motivational literature recommends. They are big, bold (some might even say overly ambitious) goals, but as study after study shows, these are the kinds of specific, numerical goals that improving and turnaround districts and schools set.

By setting such big goals, the people in these schools and districts implicitly (and sometimes explicitly in their beliefs statements) reflect a belief that their students can achieve to these high standards as well as a belief that what the school will do differently will lead to these student achievement gains. Particularly in the schools and districts with challenging demographics—high concentrations of students from lower-income, minority, and non-English-speaking back-grounds—the ambitious goals show that the faculties do not feel bound or constrained by demographics; rather, they are propelled to overcome demographics by the comprehensive and systemic nature of the curriculum and the instructional and service practices they deploy after setting these high and grand goals.

Finally, the goals in almost every instance are focused on student performance in *core subjects*, generally defined as reading/English/language arts, writing, mathematics, science, and social studies. The goals then also serve as a driver of resource allocation, as I show in subsequent chapters. When resources are scare, the deciding principle is does the proposed resource-use practice support the goal of improved student achievement in core subjects? If the proposed resource practice does not serve that goal directly, its draw on resource use takes less priority and often the idea is dropped altogether.

Setting high goals does not cost money. Yes, there needs to be a process of goal setting at the district level, which then cascades to each school and grade level or department within the school, but the process itself does not require a budget. It requires ambition, leadership, professionalism, and relentlessly pursing goal attainment.

Changing Curriculum and Defining Effective Instructional Practices

After setting ambitious goals, schools and districts change their curriculum and instructional program. They conclude that their previous programs got them to where they were and that something more rigorous and ambitious is needed to help them attain their goals.

The research does not necessarily find a consistent pattern in the kinds of new curriculum adopted, although many urban districts adopt a more structured, phonics-based reading program, and many elementary schools adopt a mathematics program with more explicit problem solving, such as *Everyday Mathematics*. If a new book series is identified for purchase before its adoption time in the normal five- to six-year textbook adoption cycle, it would require more funding, but over time, a new book series is simply absorbed into the ongoing textbook adoption budget. Ten years ago, many of the schools adopted a whole-school reform program (e.g., Stringfield, Ross, & Smith, 1996).

An increasingly specific element of this new curriculum and instructional approach, moreover, is an explicit vision of effective instructional practices. As schools and districts move toward implementing a new curriculum program, they articulate—often in quite explicit terms—the kinds of instructional practices that work in that school or district. Odden (2009) provides several specific examples of this aspect of a Plan of Action, and on reflection, it makes sense. The curriculum that is taught and the instructional approaches to teaching that curriculum (Odden, Borman, & Fermanich, 2004) are the key factors under the control of schools (and teachers) that impact student learning. Thus it makes sense that a detailed and well-articulated view of effective instructional practice would be characteristic of schools and districts moving the student achievement needle by large amounts. How this aspect of the Plan of Action can impact resource allocation is developed in subsequent chapters, especially Chapters 2 and 3.

A third element, which goes somewhat beyond what the studies reveal of school and district practices that produce large improvements in student learning, is the nature of the reading program, particularly—but not solely—the elementary reading program. The fact is that an ineffective reading program means that scores of children do not learn to read in elementary schools and have difficulty learning any subject after that. Effective reading programs include a systemic approach to teaching reading (especially for younger students coming from lower-income families), significant attention to phonemic awareness and phonics as well as word fluency, and writing and reading comprehension. In an overview of what research says about how to teach reading, I quote from a paper by Felton (2010), a reading expert working across the country:

The *four-part processor* reading model is based on scientific consensus concerning how the brain processes information for reading. This consensus is based largely on the programmatic research efforts supported by National Institute for Child Development (NICHD) beginning in 1985 with a major emphasis during the 1990s and continuing on a smaller scale today. A major finding is that reading for comprehension depends on the ability of the reader to **accurately and automatically recognize words** and attach meaning to those words. Word meaning cannot be accessed unless the word is correctly pronounced or named (e.g., sacred is not scared). Naming words correctly depends on knowledge of the sounds within words (phonemic awareness) and the way those sounds are related to print (phonics). Thus, accurate and automatic word recognition is a critical skill for reading comprehension.

There are four major processing systems that support word recognition and the brain regions involved in these have been identified. These include:

1. The **Phonological processor**—speech-sound awareness (back of the frontal lobe)

2. The **Orthographic processor**—letter and letter pattern recognition; stores printed word images (occipital region)

Note: The phonological and orthographic processors communicate to support word recognition in a region called the angular gyrus, where sound-symbol associations are processed.

3. The **Meaning processor**—also called the semantic processor— interprets word meanings in and out of context (temporal region)

4. The **Context processor**—interacts with and supports the meaning processor; gives the referent for a word's meaning (temporal areas)

All of these areas are linked and must work together for efficient reading. NICHD-sponsored research has found that the majority of students who have difficulty *learning to read do so because of difficulties in the phonological processor* system that results in inaccurate word reading skills. This is not to say that beginning readers can't have problems in the other areas, because they certainly can, but these do not comprise the majority of the poor beginning readers. Note that poor word reading skills are also an important component of reading problems for older readers, but the other processors become much more important as students progress through school and the text demands increase.

On the basis of cognitive and brain research, a "simple view of reading" has been proposed to explain the reading process. In this view, there are two major domains of reading: (1) printed word recognition and (2) language comprehension. These two domains are supported by the five components of reading that have received so much press from the National Reading Panel; i.e., (1) phonemic awareness and (2) phonics which support (3) printed word recognition and (4) vocabulary and (5) reading comprehension, which are related to language comprehension and fluency, which is important in both domains.

The following implications for beginning reading instruction derive from well-designed studies of beginning reading instruction for all students (Kindergarten through Grade 3) and are also consistent with the four processor model.

- All children should be taught *systematic, synthetic phonics* in which they are taught sound-symbol correspondences *singly, directly and explicitly*. Blending of the sound spellings should also be taught directly and explicitly until students can decode almost any unknown word. Phonemic awareness, spelling

(Continued)

(Continued)

patterns and rules, grammar, and other aspects of language structure should be taught along with phonics in an integrated fashion. Decodable readers should be used in the beginning of instruction ([Kindergarten] and Grade 1 for most students) to support the development of word recognition skills based on knowledge of language structures. Decodable readers are those that are written to provide abundant practice in reading words with the spelling patterns that are being taught (e.g., the silent-e pattern). Such readers are necessarily somewhat contrived but there exists many sources of these readers, which are entirely acceptable to children who are just learning to read. It is some teachers who have problems with such reading books because of their belief that only "authentic literature" should be used with children (see discussion below).

- All children also need exposure to rich literature, [both] fiction and non-fiction, [i.e., authentic literature], and attention to meaning, comprehension, vocabulary development, fluency and writing are essential.
- Along with developing reading skills, children's interest and pleasure in reading should be an equally important focus.

These recommendations are NOT equivalent to an eclectic combination of whole language and phonics often referred to as "balanced literacy," which is rarely truly balanced and which characterizes many reading programs around the country—and are not very effective. Classrooms that exemplify the four part processor reading model are those recommended in Reading First and Response to Intervention [RTI].

There are actually two options in choosing a core reading program. The *first* is to choose a core reading program that includes strong word identification and spelling instruction that is direct, explicit, and sequential. All aspects of language structure are taught in this way and word reading and word spelling are closely coordinated. In addition, the core has a strong intervention component that has been proven to be effective with at-risk students. The *second* option is for classrooms to continue to use a core that is acceptable in comprehension, etc., but weak in word identification and spelling and add in a separate, strong word identification/spelling program. Some separate programs are also appropriate for intervention (e.g., Fundations, Letterland) but others are not. If this option is selected, it is important for the "add-on" components to be carefully researched and used with fidelity. One of the problems seen in some schools who are using RTI is the tendency to focus intervention on separate word reading skills (e.g., letter-sound knowledge or phonemic awareness) that have been shown deficient by probes and address these in a piecemeal way (e.g., through activities at centers). A much better approach is to select *standard protocols* (i.e., programs) that address word identification and spelling difficulties in a comprehensive way rather than bit by bit.

Another important aspect of using core programs effectively is recognizing which students need modifications in the pacing of instruction. It can safely be stated that most core programs move too fast (in terms of introduction of new skills) for the 15–25% of students who are struggling with reading. What sometimes happens is that such students are provided with additional instruction (e.g., in a small group) in the skill but taught new skills at the same pace as other students. This results in such students moving on the new skills before they have mastered the old and, consequently, never mastering anything. Teachers say that they have to "cover the content" and don't really understand teaching to mastery. One approach is to help teachers understand the reason for teaching to mastery for each specific skill set and give them permission, time and the tools to do so. One example is for all students to participate in whole-group core instruction that continues at a pace appropriate for the majority of the students (this will vary according to the composition of the classroom and should be based not just on what the manual says to do on day 5 but on actual data measuring student mastery). For those students who are not mastering the content at that pace, their small-group instruction should focus on previously taught skills until they are mastered and then moving on at a slower pace. This also requires differentiating the reading materials such students are reading (e.g., providing them with appropriate readers including decodable books, to give them the reading practice necessary for mastery).

The importance of an effective reading program at all levels, but particularly in Grades K–3, cannot be overstated. All districts that have made significant improvements in student learning have addressed their reading program and restructured it to be in line with the previously mentioned research-based characteristics of effective reading programs. And a good reading program has no extra costs, because all schools and districts spend money on a reading program.

Being Strategic About Core Versus Elective Courses

Aside from class size, which the book discusses at several points, the next major fiscal decision concerns the mix between core and elective classes. To make an important point early on: this book advocates for a broad range of course offerings that would provide every student with a strong liberal arts program over their 12 to 13 years in the public school system. In addition to core classes (defined in the next paragraph), students need exposure to the arts, to physical fitness and wellness, and to emerging career-technical jobs in the evolving economy.

Core classes generally include the classes that are the foundation of the curriculum and which, in most cases, are tested at the state level: mathematics, science, reading/English/language arts/writing, history, and foreign language. Elective classes generally include art and music broadly conceived (e.g., painting, sculpture, jewelry making, chorus, band, theater), physical education/health/fitness, business, family and consumer education, and career technical education, which increasingly focuses on the health professions (e.g., nursing, doctor's assistants, medical technicians), biotechnology, and engineering. Exposure to and knowledge of the core classes usually serves as a foundation for many of the elective classes, which require knowledge of core education well into the high school years. For example, most career technical programs today require mathematical skills up to at least Algebra 2, which students usually take in the 10th or 11th grade. That is why, in part, the education goals identified today by the federal and most state governments are to prepare students to be college and career ready, with the general argument that the academic preparation for each is very much the same. This point is not to argue that all students should take AP physics; it is simply to say that achievement in core academic subjects is the foundation on which successful performance beyond high school—whether moving directly into a high-wage job or to postsecondary education—requires a substantially similar set of expertise in what are described above as core subjects.

So the first point here—and a focus for nearly all schools and districts that are dramatically improving student performance in the core subjects—is to say that all subjects need to be part of the curriculum, but some subjects (core subjects) have a higher priority than other subjects. So schools and districts moving the student achievement needle by large amounts focus resources on strategies and programs that positively and directly impact student performance in core subjects.

A related point, not emerging from the research on effective schools but being made more generally for the career component of elective classes, is the shift from the old vocational education courses (wood, metal, plastic, welding, and auto shop) to more career-technical programs in areas such as computer-aided engineering, medical technology, biotechnical programs, software and computer programming, and so on. This shift in program and course offerings not only represent a break from the former conception of career offerings but can also be implemented with lesser costs, assuming the overall resource needs of the strategies to dramatically improve performance are provided; these points are discussed in the next chapter.

Chapter 2 discusses the financial implications of how schools can be organized in various ways to provide a liberal arts program, showing that there are more and less expensive ways to accomplish this goal, which also implicitly argues that most middle schools and high schools today have adopted more expensive and less effective approaches, providing the education system with substantial ripe opportunities for resource reallocation and cost savings by reviewing their extensive elective offerings—a change that will not negatively impact student achievement in the core subjects.

To underscore these points on electives: there are no studies that find that students taking more electives do better in core classes. Electives are important; all schools improving student performance offer a broad liberal arts curriculum, which has some but not a proliferation of elective classes.

Using Data to Improve Instruction

Not only do schools and districts that are significantly improving student learning and reducing the achievement gaps not complain about state testing, but also they do not complain about too much testing, because they engage in a wide series of data-based decision-making activities, all of which require additional and more detailed information—more test data, if you will—on student academic performance, again in core subjects.

Before proceeding, this section first provides some definitions of terms that are used here and throughout the book, as there is not yet agreement on the terms to use for the variety of assessments that are given throughout the academic year in addition to the end-of-the-year state summative and accountability-focused tests. One term not used in the book is *interim assessments*, mainly because this term is used across the country to refer to any student assessment given between the annual administrations of the state summative assessments, so is too imprecise.

The book makes distinctions among screener and diagnostic assessments, formative or short cycle assessments, and benchmark assessments. Screeners generally take a short time to administer and are designed to screen students for possible problems in subjects such as reading and mathematics. If the screener suggests that the student might be at risk of reading failure or a reading problem, it is usually followed by a diagnostic test that probes, in more detail, the specific nature of the reading problem. Screeners and diagnostic assessments are used during the teaching of reading, often well into the secondary grades for students having reading problems. Northwest Evaluation Association Measures of Academic Progress (NWEA MAP), AimsWeb, and Dynamic Indicators of Basic Early Literacy Skills (DIBELS) are all examples of assessment systems that provide different versions of screener assessments.

Formative or short cycle assessments are used primarily to help teachers frame instructional practices both before a curriculum unit is taught and during the actual teaching of the unit, which is a two- to three-week period of integrated instruction designed to teach a concept in a subject area as well as its application and use. Short cycle assessments given just after a unit is taught indicate what the students in the class or grade know and don't know about the concept that was just taught and also provide background information for the next concept in the curriculum sequence; these data can be integrated with *pedagogical content knowledge*, which is knowledge already known about students vis-à-vis the concept to be taught, such as typical errors for various mathematics concepts or misconceptions for various science concepts. Short cycle assessment data are used by teacher collaborative groups to hone instructional strategies for curriculum units that the teacher teams will simultaneously teach to their classes of students.

The Wireless Generation (www.wirelessgeneration.com) provides a computerized version of formative assessments accompanied with web-based training for how the results can be used to frame instructional strategies; these assessments cover the elementary grades in reading and math, both of which are being enhanced to the middle grades in the future. Renaissance Learning STAR Enterprise assessments (www.renlearn.com/se/), available for reading and math from prekindergarten to Grade 12, are examples of short cycle assessments. The Renaissance short cycle computer-adapted assessments take a short time to administer (about 10 to 15 minutes) and are uploaded to a national database and provide immediate feedback to teachers and teacher teams.

Sometimes people use the term *formative assessment* to refer to any kind of teacher question or probe used during the actual teaching process, which provides additional and detailed information on student learning. This book does not use the term *formative assessment* for this practice, though good teachers use such probing every day they teach—a practice that obviously should continue. The book uses *formative assessments* mainly to indicate the process of getting and using student assessment data to improve the instructional process (i.e., to help frame, hone, and focus teaching to the specific learning needs of the students in the class, grade, and subject).

Benchmark assessments generally are administered on a longer cycle basis, every six to nine weeks, for example. There are many benchmark assessment systems being used across the country; one of the most popular is the MAP assessments from the Northwest Evaluation Association (NWEA). These are taken online, are computer adapted, and provide feedback to teachers, schools, and districts the day after they are administered; further, education systems can ask for their students' results to be compared to local, state, or national norms. Generally, benchmark assessments are used to track student performance progress at multiple points during the academic year; in the bulk of cases, these assessments are given at the end of the first, second, and third quarters, with state assessments being used at the end of the fourth quarter, which is the end of the year. Results from the benchmark assessments are often used to place students into various interventions or extra help programs, with the benchmark data showing that the student is making insufficient progress.

The book uses these distinctions to help clarify discussion of assessments throughout the rest of the book. At the school and district level, these distinctions are often not so clear. There are districts that administer the MAP assessments only in early September and late May but call them *formative assessments*. Used in this way, MAP assessments are not formative assessments but give a fall-to-spring change score, thus functioning as an alternative to state summative tests that provide spring-to-spring achievement changes. Short cycle assessments, if given monthly, also can be used as benchmark data, as they track progress over the course of the year; as such, they also can be used at various points to provide information about whether certain students need interventions and extra help.

Thus, the book uses *short cycle* assessments for those student performance data given prior to or just after teaching a curriculum unit, which is used to help tailor the specific instructional practices of curriculum units and interventions to the students in the class. *Benchmark* assessments are those that track practice after every quarter or every nine weeks and are used primarily for placing students into extra help programs. State tests are *summative* assessments given at the end of the year, used primarily for accountability but also, as discussed previously, used for initial analyses of the overall contours and characteristics of student performance.

Schools and districts moving the student achievement needle used a combination of short cycle (sometimes called *formative*) and benchmark assessments. The formative assessments usually were used by collaborative teacher teams to frame instructional practices that would then be used as each teacher simultaneously taught the jointly developed curriculum unit.

In addition, more recent cases of schools significantly increasing student achievement found that teachers also used *common end-of-unit tests,* thus having a comparable basis for determining how effective the unit was in producing student learning as well as for comparing student performance on the common tests across classrooms and students. In those instances where students were placed into heterogeneous classrooms, variations in classroom performance could then be explained by variations in individual teaching practice. The collaborative groups would then query the teachers whose students did well above the average, seeking to determine what else the teacher had done instructionally so those additional practices could be included in the curriculum unit the next year. The group would also provide assistance to teachers whose students lagged the average performance, and over time, put pressure on those teachers to seek jobs elsewhere—or in a different profession—if their classrooms' performances did not improve.

These schools and districts also then used benchmark data to slot students into various extra help programs, as discussed below.

But the prime point here is that the schools and districts making large positive impacts on student learning and closing achievement gaps need a range of student performance data (lots of testing data, if you will), including the following:

- short cycle assessments to hone instructional practices beforehand
- common end-of-curriculum unit tests to compare student performance results across classrooms
- benchmark assessments to guide provision of extra help services to struggling students
- end-of-year state summative assessments to assess overall progress and impact of the curriculum and instructional program

If student performance did not rise, schools and districts assumed they had gotten something wrong with the curriculum and instruction program and sought to fix it; if performance did rise, they attributed it to their hard, collaborative work and effective instructional practices.

Though there is a variety of research and case studies highlighting the importance of schools engaging in data-based decision making, a recent study of such efforts using the gold standard of research—randomized trials—showed that engaging in such decision making using interim assessment data improved student achievement in both mathematics and reading (Carlson, Borman, & Robinson, 2011).

The resource needs of formative or short cycle and benchmark assessments are not high. With $25 per pupil, schools and districts can use a wide range of such systems, including AimsWeb, the NWEA MAP assessments, Renaissance Learning STAR Enterprise assessments, and many others. Developing formative and benchmark assessments from scratch can be expensive, and few districts have done that (though most hone the systems they purchase).

Organizing Teachers Into Collaborative Groups

As already mentioned, schools and districts that impacted student performance in significant positive ways also organized teacher work in a different way than how it is currently done. Teachers were organized into collaborative instructional groups: grade-level teachers in elementary schools and subject and course groups in middle and high schools. Teachers did not work in isolation; they worked as part of collaborative teams. Using formative or short cycle assessments, the teams jointly created curriculum units, which all teachers in the team taught, usually simultaneously; the teams then also administered the same end-of-unit test so student performance could be compared across all classrooms. Over the course of the year, the members of the team might visit a class where the teacher was producing above-average classroom performance or having more success with struggling learners; struggling team members would also receive visits and assistance from both other members of the team as well as instructional coaches (discussed below).

The point here: teachers did not work on their own *and* viewed instructional practice as something that was jointly developed and systemically implemented. They believed that a more common approach to teaching—mentioned earlier as an articulation of instructional practices that worked with their students in their schools—was critical to the performance success of their students, and they put professional pressure on all teachers to get with the school's instructional program.

This more-systemic approach to the provision of instruction squares with emerging research on how to impact student performance and reduce achievement gaps. As Steve Raudenbusch (2009) argued in a recent research analysis, the education system knows how to raise overall achievement and close the achievement gaps. *First,* he argued, there is strong evidence, from a wide variety of research studies, that teacher effectiveness varies substantially across classrooms and that the major reasons for the variation are differences in a teacher's instructional practice. *Second,* the way to reduce the variation in teacher effectiveness—to make teacher effectiveness more constant across classrooms, if you will—is to identify the core features of effective instructional practice and get that kind of instruction consistently implemented in all classrooms. And *third,* the way to attain that latter objective is to change the culture of schools from viewing instruction as individualistic, autonomous, private, and more idiosyncratic to individual teachers who use their own strategies and assessment items, to viewing instruction as more systemic, public, and professional and as something that grows from collaborative work using common instructional strategies and more common assessment tasks.

Principals and the teachers in the effective schools held the above suppositions and also believed that the way to change culture in a school and get a more uniform deployment of effective instructional practice into all classrooms was to organize teachers into collaborative teams to work together on an ongoing basis using student data to engage in the cycle of continuous instructional improvement. Their vision was to see teachers working in collaborative groups, sometimes called Professional Learning Communities (PLCs), using student data to constantly improve teaching practice while focusing on both individual and class learning needs.

Further, to facilitate this teacher work, there needs to be at least four items available for each core subject:

- a set of individual short cycle or formative assessments for each curriculum unit (and for discussion, let's assume that a *curriculum unit* is three to four weeks of instruction during which students learn a specific concept)
- common end-of-curriculum unit assessments (which would show the learning of each student and, when aggregated, could show the learning of each class of students)
- common quarterly or benchmark assessments given every nine weeks
- state summative tests

All of these were identified in the previous section as key elements of the Plan of Action in the effective schools and districts studied.

Put a different way, teachers were organized into collaborative teams as a way both to reduce teacher isolation in schools and to change the school culture from instruction seen as idiosyncratic to individual teachers to instruction viewed as more collegial and systemically deployed by all teachers. Faculties believed that this was the way both to improve student performance overall and to reduce achievement gaps—results that all these schools attained. Faculties further believed that this was the way to provide all students—especially students from low-income and minority backgrounds—high-quality instruction as the foundation from which extra help services, if needed, would evolve.

Once a school is staffed, organizing teachers into collaborative groups requires no additional resources. It does entail paying attention to the school schedule and ensuring that all teachers in each collaborative team have at least some time during the day, if not during the week, to engage in the collaboration described earlier—I suggest at least three 45-minute periods a week.

Investing in Ongoing, Comprehensive, and Intensive Professional Development

Analyzing state summative data to determine the existing performance situation, using formative data to hone instructional practice before it is deployed, working effectively in collaborative teams, and implementing new curriculum and instructional programs all require new knowledge and skills, so schools and districts that moved the student achievement needle by large increments engaged all teachers in ongoing, comprehensive, and intensive professional development.

The professional development often included two-week (or longer) summer institutes, shorter training sessions during the school year, and substantial collaborative work during the school day and week on the details of curriculum and instructional practice as well as work with instructional coaches. Instructional coaches, with multiple and various labels—coach, mentor, facilitator, professional development teacher, lead teacher, content expert, and so on—work with teachers in collaborative groups (often helping them analyze the instructional implications of the formative data from 25 students in a class or 125 students in a grade), use benchmark data to place student into appropriate interventions, and understand the instructional implications of screeners and diagnostic assessments as well as modeling effective instructional practices in individual teachers' classrooms.

A recent randomized trial study of coaching found significant, positive impacts of student achievement gains across four subject areas—mathematics, science, history, and language arts (Pianta, Allen, & King, 2011), thus supporting this expensive element of the Plan of Action with research findings derived from the gold standard of research.

This professional development was not viewed as once and done but as an ongoing element of the school's program and as critical to the goal of getting more effective instructional practices more consistently deployed in all classrooms, which is the foundational strategy for improving student performance. Further, these approaches to professional development needed resources—non-pupil days for training, non-pupil periods during the regular school day for collaborative work, and funds for trainers and school-based instructional coaches.

Extra Help for Students Struggling to Meet Rigorous Performance Standards

Though the leading objective was to have every teacher deploy the highest-quality and most effective instructional practices as the core and foundational instructional treatment for all students, faculties and administrators in these schools also knew that no matter how excellent and effective core instruction could be, there would also be some students—in some classrooms, a substantial number of students—that would need extra help in order to achieve to proficiency if not advanced standards. Thus, the schools created and implemented a variety of extra help strategies.

Without getting into the formal definition of the term, at a general level, the schools implemented a Response to Intervention (RTI) approach to providing the full array of services that all students need. The first need was for the highest-quality core instruction to be provided to every student (except, of course, those students with multiple, severe, and profound disabilities, who were taught in separate classrooms). The second need was for classroom accommodations that could be provided by the regular teacher. Both were consider Tier 1 interventions in the RTI framework.

But these schools then followed the highest-quality Tier 1 work with a set of Tier 2 and Tier 3 services. Their Plan of Action was to expand instructional time and hold performance expectations steady for all students. Tier 2 consisted of a range of extra help strategies:

- extra help during the regular school day, including one-to-one tutoring for students with the most difficult learning problems as well as small groups (three to five students) for those with less difficult learning issues (which aligns well with the elements of interventions included in effective reading programs)

- extra help during the regular school year but outside of the regular school day, providing academic help in various forms before school, after school, and Saturday extended-day programs
- extra help outside of the regular school day and regular school year in summer school services

The combination of these extra help programs varied widely, with no common patterns except that schools that provided at least some one-to-one tutoring had strong, positive success with that intervention; related research shows that such intensive early intervention (also including small-group tutoring for groups up to a maximum of five students) can also reduce the incidence of students needing a "label" of being a student with a disability and a related Individualized Education Program (IEP) (Levenson, 2011).

These extra help services require substantial resources, the details of which will be discussed in Chapter 2. Since the bulk of students struggling to achieve to high performance levels are from lower-income backgrounds and non-English-speaking families, providing the resources to schools to provide these resources mean districts (as well as states and the federal government) must allocate resources in an unequal but equitable manner; schools with more students from poverty backgrounds and more English language learner (ELL) students should receive more resources so these extra help programs can be funded. This is precisely the initial message Superintendent Weast made in Montgomery Country—the district's demographics were changing, and unless the district recognized these changes and changed how it allocated overall resources, the schools with the new demographic of students would not have the resources to meet their students' performance needs and challenges.

Distributing Leadership Across All Levels and All Roles

As readers have already surmised, leadership in these schools and districts was not provided by just administrators; there was both a *density* of leadership (many leaders) and a *dispersion* of leadership (leaders at all levels) within the system, particularly in the school. Some might call this *distributed* leadership (see Spillane, 2006). The collaborative teacher teams were usually coordinated by a lead teacher who provided leadership at the team level. Instructional coaches, in addition to principals, provided leadership at the school level. Central office administrators often conducted school walk-throughs, observing instructional practice and curriculum and text-book implementation and providing leadership from another location in the education system. The districts that moved student achievement upward had strong, performance-oriented superintendents as well as strong leaders in the academic and professional development divisions and, increasingly, in the human resource management divisions. Leadership also came from some—but not all—budget and fiscal divisions; this book hopefully will provide those fiscal leaders with ideas and fiscal strategies that empower them to contribute as much to instructional change as these other leaders by strategically deploying budget resources.

Assuming districts and schools have an appropriate array of individuals in leadership or coordination positions, leadership density and distributed instructional leadership are not additional cost items; they are approaches that define what individuals in leadership roles do.

Creating a Professional Culture

All of the schools and districts improving student achievement and reducing the achievement gaps created what the literature calls *professional school cultures* (e.g., Louis & Marks, 1998; Marks & Louis, 1997; Newmann & Associates, 1996). Professional school cultures are characterized by the following traits:

- common high expectations for the learning of all students
- common understandings of effective instruction and a systemic approach to deploying these instructional practices, often called the *deprivatization* of instructional practice
- teacher and administrator responsibility for student achievement results

As should be clear, these principles characterized these schools and districts. Additionally, the faculties and administrators in these schools keep abreast of ongoing educational research—looking for articles on what works—with both teachers and administrators bringing articles to school for everyone to read and discuss. Further, many also engaged in a continuous search for the best practices, whether those emerged from the more effective teachers in their own schools, from school practices in similar schools within the district, or from benchmarking with other schools and districts across the region or state.

These educators were professionals—they wanted to deploy the best, most up-to-date instructional practices in their school. They believed that doing this was the key to improving student performance. They believed that when performance rose, it was because of what occurred instructionally in classrooms. They believed that when student performance did not rise, or when various student groups did not keep up, the glitches were in the instructional programs, not the students, and then set out to find and repair the instructional shortcomings.

Taking Teacher and Principal Talent Seriously

The importance of teacher and principal talent is a more recent element of schools and districts turning around, boosting student performance, and reducing the achievement gaps (see Chapter 4 and Odden, 2011a). The experience of Hamilton County in Chattanooga, Tennessee, was a forerunner of this issue (Chenoweth, 2007). When the Chattanooga city school system, which had a concentration of students from low-income and poverty backgrounds, merged with the Hamilton County school system, leaders concluded that overall the teachers and principals from Chattanooga were not as effective as those in the surrounding country and were a major factor in the lower education achievement of the students in the city schools. Thus, through multiple initiatives, including some top-down decisions and other incentives, the merged district moved out the teachers and principals in the city's lowest-performing schools and brought in new principals, who were able to select the new faculties. Combined with changes in the curriculum program and intensive professional development, these human capital changes were major factors in the improvement in most of these schools.

Odden (2011a) shows how changes in teacher and principal talent also have been a key element of improved student performance in many of the urban districts around the country, including Atlanta, Boston, Chicago, Long Beach, and New York City, and have become a key element of new federal education initiatives, particularly those in the new competitive grant programs (e.g., Race to the Top, School Improvement, Innovation Fund).

The point here is that while a comprehensive and multifaceted education improvement strategy is needed, effective teachers and principals are also needed to successfully implement the strategy. Often, districts and schools must take a hard look at their existing talent pool and decide if it is up to the task and, if it is not, decide what human capital strategies are needed to provide the requisite talent. This issue is so important that a separate chapter of the book—Chapter 4—is devoted to this topic.

Though there are some costs associated with acquiring, developing, motivating, and retaining top teacher and principal talent, the bulk of school district budgets is spent on staff, so generally, this element requires just a few additional resources—it primarily represents a different and more deliberate way to recruit smarter, more able, and more effective individuals into the lower-performing schools that need them the most as well as to move out those in the system that are not effective.

Embracing a Performance Culture of Accountability for Student Achievement Results

The last core element of the set of strategies schools and districts deploy to dramatically improve student performance and close the achievement gaps is creating a performance- and accountability-oriented culture. In many ways, this point already has been implicitly made, but it is wise to make it explicit. These schools are aggressively and relentlessly performance oriented—they want to boost student performance and will do whatever it takes to accomplish that core goal. They do not blame parents, political leaders, external events, or even budget shortages for lack of gains in student performance; if performance gains do not improve, they blame themselves. In short, they take professional responsibility for the results of their instructional practices.

As a result, they were rarely fazed by external accountability requirements, whether it was the flawed requirements for adequate yearly progress (AYP) under the federal No Child Left Behind (NCLB) program or any state accountability initiative. One reason was these schools and districts tended to meet those accountability requirements in part because their goals were much more aggressive than even AYP goals under NCLB. And if they did not meet them, they tried to figure out why and, if possible, to remedy the shortcoming in their instructional program.

In these ways, the educators in these effective schools displayed many of the characteristics and instructional approaches of the most effective teachers in the Teach For America program (Farr, 2010). They set very ambitious goals, and they focused all energies and resources toward attaining those goals; thus, being performance driven and accepting responsibility for results, they were comfortable with accountability for those results.

Summary

There are scores of examples of schools and districts across the United States that have dramatically improved student performance on state tests over a four- to six-year period. Further, there is a remarkable similarity in the overall strategies that such schools and districts have deployed:

- They analyze state test scores to determine their current performance situation.
- They set very high and ambitious (sometimes "eye-popping") goals for student performance.
- They change curriculum programs, define their version of effective instructional practices, and implement structured, systemic, and research-based reading programs. They also make sure the reading program at all levels is sound and works; an effective reading program is crucial for student learning in all subjects.
- They are strategic about the number of core versus elective courses.
- They use short cycle, benchmark, and common end-of-curriculum unit student assessment data to improve instruction.
- They provide appropriate interventions for struggling students.
- They organize teachers into collaborative groups.
- They invest in ongoing, comprehensive, and intensive professional development.
- They implement multiple strategies to help struggling students meet rigorous performance standards.
- They distribute leadership—for both teachers and administrators—across all school levels and all roles.
- They create a professional culture.
- They take the acquisition, development, and retention of teacher and principal talent seriously.
- They embrace a culture of accountability for student achievement results.

Finally, as noted in the text, there are increasing numbers of randomized trial experiments—the gold standard of research—that document the individual elements of this comprehensive Plan of Action. Further, in addition to the case studies cited at the beginning of this chapter (and from which the chapter draws), there are now randomized trials of the effects of comprehensive whole-school approaches to improving student performance (see, for example, Borman et al., 2007). Put differently, the promise presented by case studies is now being more firmly documented by randomized trial research findings, both on the individual program elements of the Plan of Action and the Plan of Action as a whole. I would call this good news.

Note

1. More detail on all the points, specific school and district examples, and more research citations can be found in my most recent books: Odden (2009), Odden and Archibald (2009), and Odden (2011a).

2

The Resource Needs of the Plan of Action

- In 2004, the Arkansas legislature enacted a new school funding formula that included the bulk of resources in the Plan of Action described in Chapter 1, including all the resources for comprehensive professional development.
- In 2006, the Wyoming legislature enacted a new school funding formula that included all the resources in the Plan of Action described in Chapter 1.
- In 2009, the South Dakota legislature enacted a new school funding formula that also included the bulk of resources in Chapter 1's Plan of Action.

In sum, state legislatures are willing to enhance education funding on the basis of a comprehensive Plan of Action designed to boost student learning and a clear and specific delineation of the resource needs of that plan.

The resources for all the programmatic elements of the Plan of Action discussed in Chapter 1 are not insubstantial. Not all school districts have all the resources needed to implement all the elements outlined in the Plan of Action. This chapter identifies in specific terms those resource needs—in both staffing requirements and dollar amounts. The various cases and studies of these improving schools and districts provide us with sufficient detail to identify the major programmatic elements of the different strategies (and thus the major categories where resources are needed).

Because the schools and districts that have improved performance did not necessarily do so in all areas or at every grade or school, we cannot discern from them what the total costs of producing such performance gains would be. Thus, this chapter also draws from work on school finance adequacy—conducted through Lawrence O. Picus and Associates—to specify resource levels in areas that are somewhat more ambiguous than the data produced by case studies of dramatic improvement. This chapter identifies resource needs for the Plan of Action described in Chapter 1 at a level that should be considered adequate—which is to say, sufficient to enable schools to significantly improve the performance of all students, what I have called in other contexts *doubling* student performance on state summative tests (Odden, 2009; Odden & Archibald, 2009).

The research—both on specific programs and on case studies of districts and schools that are improving performance—that supports the suggested level of resources can be found in the school finance text I have written with Lawrence O. Picus (Odden & Picus, 2008) and various school finance adequacy studies we have conducted (see www.lpicus.com). Nearly every adequacy study also includes studies of schools and districts with improving performance and shows how the resource categories in the finance analyses are tightly aligned with the resource categories of the case studies.

Put a different way, the initially suggested staffing and resource levels are good approximations of what can be considered an adequate set of staffing and dollar resources (Odden, Goetz, & Picus, 2010; Odden, Picus, & Goetz, 2010). They are a specific and concrete place to begin thinking about strategic resource allocation. If budgets are lower than the suggested level, then cutbacks can be made in ways that first retain the most important of the programmatic elements of the Plan of Action (those with the largest impacts on student learning gains in core subjects); then, if necessary, even those elements can be pared back to a budget level that can be afforded. If budgets are higher than suggested (which is the case in many education systems), states, districts, and schools could use the suggested level of resources as guideposts for where and how bigger funding cuts could be made without harming student performance.

At the same time the book articulates these caveats, as Chapter 1 also showed, there are increasing numbers of randomized controlled trial studies of not only the individual elements of the Plan of Action but of all the elements of the Plan put together and implemented. So though the elements of the Plan of Action are certainly not absolute truths, there is considerable and growing research evidence that these strategies do indeed work.

Details of the Resource Needs of the Plan of Action

The suggestions for the specific resource needs of all the programmatic elements discussed in Chapter 1, as well as other aspects of schools that need to be resourced, include the following (again, see Odden, 2009, as well as Chapter 4 of Odden & Picus, 2008, for more evidence supporting each of these recommendations):

1. Full day kindergarten. See Fusaro (1997) for a meta-analysis of research on the effects of full-day kindergarten on achievement.

2. Core class sizes of 15 students for Grades K–3 and class sizes of 25 students for all Grades 4–12. *Core* is defined as the regular classroom teacher in elementary schools and teachers of mathematics, science, reading/English/writing, history, and foreign language in secondary schools. With these ratios, class sizes average 18 students in the elementary school and 25 students in middle and high schools. See Finn and Achilles (1999) for randomized trial evidence of the effects of class sizes of 15 students in Grades K–3 and Konstantopoulos and Chung (2009) for long-term effects as well.

3. Specialist teachers to provide instruction in art, music, physical education, career technical education, and so on in numbers adequate to cover a six-period day in middle schools with teachers teaching for just five periods and four 90-minute block schedules in high schools with teachers teaching for just three blocks each day.

4. At least one period (45 to 60 minutes) of planning and preparation time each day for all teachers in elementary, middle, and high schools. The next chapter discusses how to go one

step further and provide for teacher collaborative time as well, with no extra cost.

5. Pupil support staff, including guidance counselors (1 full-time equivalent [FTE] position for every 250 students in middle and high schools) and nurses as well as additional pupil support (including social workers and family liaison personnel), the latter provided on the basis of 1 position for every 100 at-risk students, with a minimum of one person in every prototypical elementary school.[1]

6. A full-time librarian and principal in every prototypical school as well as two secretarial positions in a prototypical elementary (432 students) and middle school (450 students), three secretaries in a prototypical high school (600 students), and sometimes an additional assistant principal in the prototypical high school.

7. An ambitious set of professional development resources, including one instructional coach for every 200 students (three FTE positions in a 600-student high school), at least 10 pupil-free days for professional development (which usually means extending the teacher school year of 180 days of instruction by several additional days), and $100/pupil for trainers and other expenses related to professional development as well as the above allocations for elective teachers, which together with core teachers allows schools to create 45 to 60 minutes each day that is pupil free and can be used for teacher collaborative work. See Pianta, Allan, and King (2011) for randomized trial evidence on coaching.

8. Supervisory aides to cover recess, lunch, hall monitoring, and bus loading and unloading.

9. About $175 per pupil for instructional materials, formative assessments, and supplies; $250 per pupil for technology and equipment; and $250 per pupil for student activities (sports, clubs, etc.). See Carlson, Borman, and Robinson (2011) for randomized trial evidence on data-based decision making.

10. $25 per pupil to provide extra strategies for gifted and talented students.

11. A comprehensive range of extra help and Tier 2 intervention strategies for students who need additional instructional

assistance and extra time to achieve to rigorous state proficiency standards including:

a. Resources to provide one-to-one tutoring at the ratio of one teacher/tutor position for every 100 at-risk students, with a minimum of one position for every prototypical school. See Torgeson (2004) for an overview of randomized trial evidence on the effects of one-to-one tutoring and small-group (one to five students per group) tutoring interventions and Bloom (1984) for the seminal study of tutoring effects.

b. Extended-day resources to provide an eight- to nine-week summer program of up to six hours per day of academic help, at the ratio of one teacher position for every 30 at-risk students, assuming that only about 50 percent of at-risk students would participate, so class sizes consist of 15 students. See Patall, Cooper, and Allen (2011) for evidence on effective extended-day programs and what makes them work.

c. Summer school resources to provide a summer program for up to six hours a day for eight to nine weeks and academic help for two-thirds of the summer, at the ratio of one teacher position for every 30 at-risk students, assuming that only about 50 percent of at-risk students would need such extra help and would attend the program, so class sizes consist of 15 students. See Borman and Dowling (2006) for randomized trial evidence of the long-term effects of summer school and Cooper, Charlton, Valentine, and Muhlenbruck (2000) for a meta-analysis of summer school effects.

d. One additional teacher position for every 100 English language learning (ELL) students (the bulk of whom also are at risk and trigger the first three extra help resources), primarily to provide instruction in English as a second language. See Slavin, Madden, Calderon, Chamberlain, & Hennessy (2011) for randomized trial research on the effects of bilingual education.

e. One teacher and 0.5 aide position for every 150 students to provide services to students with mild and moderate disabilities (three certified positions for a 450-student elementary school or middle school and four certified positions for a 600-student high school). The model also advocates full state funding of the entire cost of the high-cost special-need students (assuming 2 percent of those with disabilities are in the high-cost category).

12. Substitute teacher resources at 10 days for each teacher and instructional facilitator position.

13. Central office staff covering the superintendent's office, the business office, curriculum and pupil support, technology personnel and an operations and maintenance director (a per-pupil figure derived from a prototypical 3,500 student district).

14. Additional resources for operations and maintenance, transportation, and food services.

To show what all these core recommendations mean in terms of staff positions and dollars, the recommendations are displayed as applied to prototypical elementary, middle, and high schools (see Table 2.1). However, in actual use, the core recommendations are tailored to the student numbers and student demographics of each school in a district, so schools with more students than shown in the prototypical schools would have proportionately more resources, and schools with fewer students would receive fewer resources, though several core resources—principal, secretary, librarian—often are retained for smaller schools to address diseconomies of small school size. Further, schools with larger (or smaller) concentrations and numbers of at-risk students as compared to the illustrative figures in Table 2.1 of 50 percent poverty and 10.6 percent ELL would be eligible for a greater (or lesser) level of resources triggered by those higher (or lower) pupil counts.

The specific prototypical school sizes in Table 2.1 are simply illustrative examples to show how the staffing formulas would work in specific schools; state or district policymakers could change the size of prototypical schools as well as the specific staffing formulas themselves. The formulas are starting points—evidence- and best-practice-based starting points—for both analyses of school finance adequacy conducted for state leaders and strategic budgeting studies conducted for district and school leaders.

Since there does not exist today (nor will there exist in the future) any pure science to what the staffing formula and dollar-per-pupil resource levels should be, the above formulas and recommendations (as stated earlier) are good approximations of specific resource needs. They are a solid place to begin deliberations—many with considerable research supporting their specifics. They help to frame a beginning point from which to launch strategic budgeting exercises.

(Text continues on p. 39.)

Table 2.1 Suggested Staffing and Resource Levels for Prototypical Elementary, Middle, and High Schools

School Element	Elementary Schools	Middle Schools	High Schools
School Characteristics			
School configuration	Kindergarten–Grade 5	Grades 6–8	Grades 9–12
Prototypical school size	432	450	600
Class size	Kindergarten–Grade 3: 15; Grades 4–5: 25	Grades 6–8: 25	Grades 9–12: 25
Full day kindergarten	Yes	NA	NA
Number of teacher workdays	195 teacher workdays, including 10 days for professional development	190 teacher workdays, including 10 days for professional development	190 teacher workdays, including 10 days for professional development
Percentage of students from poverty backgrounds (free and reduced lunch) for illustrative purposes only	50%	50%	50%
Percentage of ELL students for illustrative purposes only	10.6%	10.6%	10.6%

(Continued)

Table 2.1   *(Continued)*

School Element	Elementary Schools	Middle Schools	High Schools
Personnel Resources			
1. Core teachers	24	18	24
2. Specialist teachers	20% of core teacher figures, assuming a six-period day; teachers teach 5 periods daily: 4.8	20% of core teacher figures, assuming a six-period day; teachers teach 5 periods daily: 3.6	33% of core teacher figures, assuming a 90-minute block schedule; teachers teach 3 blocks daily: 8.0
3. Instructional facilitators/ coaches	One for every 200 students: 2.2	One for every 200 students: 2.25	One for every 200 students: 3.0
4. Tier 2: Tutors for struggling students	One for every 100 poverty students, with a minimum of 1 for each school: 2.16	One for every 100 poverty students, with a minimum of 1 for each school: 2.25	One for every 100 poverty students, with minimum of 1 for each school: 3.00
5. Tier 2: Teachers for ELL students	One additional teacher for every 100 ELL students: 0.46	One additional teacher for every 100 ELL students: 0.48	One additional teacher for every 100 ELL students: 0.64
6. Tier 2: Extended-day schooling	1.8 teachers	1.875 teachers	2.5 teachers
7. Tier 2: Summer school	1.8 teachers	1.875 teachers	2.5 teachers

Table 2.1

School Element	Elementary Schools	Middle Schools	High Schools
8. Students with mild disabilities	Additional 3 professional teacher positions and 1.5 aide positions	Additional 3 professional teacher positions and 1.5 aide positions	Additional 4 professional teacher positions and 2.0 aide positions
9. Students with severe disabilities	100% state reimbursement minus federal funds	100% state reimbursement minus federal funds	100% state reimbursement minus federal funds
10. Resources for gifted/talented students	$25/student	$25/student	$25/student
11. Substitutes	10 days for each teacher	10 days for each teacher	10 days for each teacher
12. Pupil support staff	One for every 100 students with poverty backgrounds, with minimum of 1 per school: 1.32	One for every 100 students with poverty backgrounds, plus 1 guidance staff per 250 students: 3.18 total	One for every 100 students with poverty backgrounds, plus 1 guidance staff per 250 students: 4.25 total
13. Supervisory aides	2	2	3
14. Librarian	1	1	1
15. Principal	1 (plus assistant principals in larger schools)	1 (plus assistant principals in larger schools)	1 (plus assistant principals in larger schools)
16. School site secretary	1 secretary 1 clerk	1 secretary 1 clerk	1 secretary 3 clerks

(Continued)

Table 2.1 *(Continued)*

School Element	Elementary Schools	Middle Schools	High Schools
Dollars Per Pupil			
17. Professional development	*Included above:* Instructional facilitators 10 summer days for training *Additional:* $100/pupil for other professional development expenses— trainers, conferences, travel, and so on	*Included above:* Instructional facilitators 10 summer days for training *Additional:* $100/pupil for other professional development expenses— trainers, conferences, travel, and so on	*Included above:* Instructional facilitators 10 summer days for training *Additional:* $100/pupil for other professional development expenses— trainers, conferences, travel, and so on
18. Technology/ equipment	$250/pupil	$250/pupil	$250/pupil
19. Instructional materials and formative assessments	$165/pupil	$165/pupil	$200/pupil
20. Student activities	$250/pupil	$250/pupil	$250/pupil
Other Expenditures			
21. Central office	A $/pupil figure	A $/pupil figure	A $/pupil figure
22. Operations and maintenance	A $/pupil figure	A $/pupil figure	A $/pupil figure
23. Transportation	A $/pupil figure	A $/pupil figure	A $/pupil figure
24. Food services	A $/pupil figure	A $/pupil figure	A $/pupil figure

NA = Not applicable
ELL = English language learner

It also should be noted that, from a school finance adequacy perspective, state policymakers can enhance or reduce any of the specific
formulas, at least to some degree. And nearly all states in which
I have worked have done just that, and their decisions, even when
modestly reducing the total resources, have been supported by subsequent state Supreme Court decisions.

These staffing and resource levels can also serve as guide posts for
local districts and schools beginning a process of strategic budgeting.
Where the resources tailored to a specific school in Table 2.1 are less
than those of what the district actually provides, the district and school
staff are given information that resources in those categories could be
reduced if the budget needed to be cut or shifted to other categories
where there might be resource shortages. Where the resources tailored
to a specific school in Table 2.1 exceed those of what the district provided, the district and schools staff are given information that resources
in those categories should be increased, if fiscally possible—initially via
resource reallocation. If there are categories where the school has simply been allocated no resources, Table 2.1 would indicate that that is an
area that needs immediate resourcing attention—even if the budget
does not allow fully resourcing such a category currently.

In short, Table 2.1 can give states, districts, and schools a starting
point for strategic fiscal analyses. It firstly indicates all the categories
where there should be resources. I have worked with districts where
the category of "teacher/tutors" is blank for all schools, and upon
reviewing the data in a district-specific Table 2.1, district leaders
immediately decided that teacher/tutors—the most powerful type of
Tier 2 intervention—was a staffing resource that needed to be
increased. Such districts often started by allocating at least one such
position to each school. Secondly, a district-tailored Table 1, as stated
earlier, also gives the district an external framework for assessing
how it actually provides resources. I have worked in several districts
that provided smaller class sizes than suggested by the table; as a
result, saving resources by increasing those class sizes immediately
became a possibility, and using the saved teacher resources either cut
budgets or staffed under-resourced areas, which usually include
instructional coaches and teacher/tutors.

Finally, I have worked in districts that simply had fewer resources
in every single category of Table 2.1. In some of those districts, the
Table engendered bitterness—the reaction of "What can we do? We
don't have sufficient resources." In other districts that had fewer
resources than Table 2.1 indicates, the resource shortage simply
showed them that their challenge was harder and that they had to do
more with less. In these districts, the necessity of having larger class

sizes was not seen as an impediment to making progress in boosting student learning. Moreover, some of these districts even were willing to further increase class sizes to produce staffing positions for instructional coaches and teacher/tutors or to carve out time for collaborative teacher work, concluding that those latter strategies would have a much larger positive impact on student achievement than would reducing class sizes by one to three students.

Example of a High-Spending District That Could Cut Spending

I have a close friend who was on the school board of a suburban district in the New York City metropolitan area. Several years ago, the district was facing a budget shortage. She knew I had some expertise in this topic and asked me for advice. I asked for staffing charts for several of the schools in the districts. In the elementary schools, I found the following:

- class sizes around 20 students
- elective teachers that exceeded 20 percent of core teachers
- assistant principals provided to schools of 400 students (and, of course, double that for a school of 800)
- substantial numbers of instructional coaches
- three or so student support staff including guidance counselors, social workers, and so on
- four to six extra help staff for struggling students, providing a wide variety of services
- extensive numbers of special education teachers and instructional aides
- instructional aides in addition to those in the special education program
- one period a day for individual planning time and another for teacher collaborative work, with teachers organized into professional learning communities
- large budgets for instructional materials

Similar high levels of staffing and dollar resources were provided to the district's middle and high schools, with the numbers of elective teachers in high schools almost equaling those of core teachers.

In sum, what I found was that this district was staffing its schools *in virtually every category* at a rate substantially above what would be suggested from the formulas behind Table 2.1. So I told her that there were multiple places where they could cut their budgets. I also told her that such actions might have a negative political backlash as it would make the district an oddball in their broader community—their district would provide schools with fewer resources than their surrounding districts. Nevertheless, from what I would call a pretty strong evidence base, the district (and probably the state) had substantial leeway to cut its budget in ways that would have virtually no negative impact on student learning, because the district had already provided more resources than were necessary.

Linking Table 2.1 to School Finance Adequacy

The staffing and dollar-per-pupil suggestions in the previous section can serve and have served as the basis for determining an adequate education spending level in any state. In Arkansas, the data were used to construct a new statewide foundation expenditure level, with additional categorical programs for the resources triggered by poverty and ELL student counts. This approach hides the allocations of the foundation dollars by the various staffing and resource categories in Table 2.1. Wyoming, on the other hand, incorporated the school-based staffing allocations into its revised funding formula, together with multiple—and substantial—adjustments for small school and district size. So there are multiple ways states can use the specific resource recommendations embodied in Table 2.1 to redesign state school funding structures.

We have also used the Arkansas approach to determine on a national average basis what an adequate per-pupil spending level would be, including adjustments for struggling students, ELL students, and students with a disability (Odden, Goetz et al., 2010; Odden, Picus et al., 2010). We found that, on average, the country is very close to providing adequate resources for schools, although some portions of the country provide much less than do others. But this study showed that if the country took a more national perspective of how it would fund its schools—like it is taking with adopting Common Math and Reading Standards and the understanding that good education is key to the *country's* economic health—it would not have to provide much more funding to ensure an adequate level of resources in all schools.

In a subsequent study (Odden, Picus et al., 2010), we tailored the recommendations and formulas in Table 2.1 to the demographics and student numbers in each of the 50 states. We found that a score of states—including Connecticut, New Hampshire, New Jersey, and New York—already provided resources significantly above those implied by a state-specific version of Table 2.1. This should give schools and districts in those states some comfort if they are forced to cut their budgets; if they use the formulas in Table 2.1 as guideposts, they could cut budgets to the levels suggested. And we would argue that such strategic cuts, which would keep all resources at or above the levels in their specific category in Table 2.1, would have no impact on their students' performance.

The study also showed a score of states—including Alabama, Arizona, California, Florida, Georgia, Mississippi, Tennessee, Texas, and Utah—had funding below the level suggested by their state-tailored version of Table 2.1. Thus, it will be more difficult to cut school budgets in those states, although the following chapters will indicate how they can make such cuts in strategic ways that could have them continue on their paths of improving student learning. But each of those states could use the formulas and resource levels included in Table 2.1 as a rationale for why, over time, education funding should be increased and for what resources.

The data for the above study would need to be updated to a 2011-base to see how the results would look today, as most education budgets have been cut or inflation-eroded during the past two years. And of course, the overall state result would be different for each district in the state. New York, for example, has many districts spending both above and below the state average; so in any final analysis, the situation would vary by district and by school. But that study showed that the suggested staffing and dollar levels in a state-, district-, or school-tailored Table 2.1 would be much easier to provide or maintain in some places but much more difficult in others, with the latter facing more complex strategic budgeting decisions.

Summary

The staffing and dollar-per-pupil figures suggested in Table 2.1 identify a foundational level of resources needed by all schools if they are to boost student achievement to new high levels. It also is the case that some schools today have more than the recommended levels of resources and other schools have less than those amounts. Still other schools have more in some categories and less in others. And some schools and districts have less in all categories and so face more difficult funding challenges. The data in Table 2.1 also can and have been used to restructure state school-funding formulas to ensure that all districts and schools have adequate resources. The next chapter shows in more detail how the recommendations in Table 2.1 can be used by any district to reallocate extant resources to strategies that are likely to be more effective as a response to performance improvement challenges. Indeed, Chapters 3 and 6 argue that the resource structure in Table 2.1 can serve as a starting point for any school deciding how best to use its staffing resources, whether starting from a position with more or fewer resources than those in Table 2.1.

Note

1. At-risk students are generally the number of students eligible for the federal free and reduced-price lunch program, with adjustments for high school students where lunch eligibility is typically underreported.

3

Targeting Resources to Student Learning When Budgets Are Tight[1]

- Beaverton (OR) used the template of resources in Chapter 1's Plan of Action as a guide for how it could cut its budget and still enhance core instruction to boost student learning. All its educators were quite flexible about class size as the district sought to provide collaborative planning time for all teachers as well as instructional coaches to enhance the effectiveness of core instruction.
- The KnowledgeWorks Foundation funded several Ohio districts—one urban, one suburban, and one rural—in 2010 as they worked together to identify strategies to reduce budgets in ways that retained key elements of the Plan of Action as each district was under the gun to also improve student learning.
- Des Moines (IA) reduced the number of high school administrators in order to place instructional coaches in each high school as a strategy to improve core instructional practice.

For over a decade, numerous schools and districts across the country have been reallocating resources to those in the Plan of Action as part of their efforts to boost student learning with the funds they have.

Yes, education budgets today are imploding at the fiscal seams. A sluggish economy and falling property values are shortchanging public education budgets across the country. At the same time, expectations for improved student performance, better teachers, and closing the achievement gap continue to grow. Schools and teachers are caught in this double squeeze.

I have concluded there are ways to move forward through this fiscal squeeze. Schools can improve learning and teaching using research- and best-practice-based strategies that, in many cases, do not require more money but the reallocation of existing resources. Over time, some schools will need more money, but in the near-to-medium future, all schools can make progress with the funds currently in their systems.

But there are competing views about this dilemma. One group argues that more competition will ensure that schools spend education dollars more efficiently and that the demands on schools today require more choice—vouchers, charter schools, contract schools, and other market-driven solutions. Some who support competition also want to give schools more control over spending decisions. These approaches have merit, but competition *per se* won't improve schools. After all, two of America's automobile manufacturing companies went bankrupt while operating in competitive markets. To survive and compete in a vastly different marketplace, they had to redesign and improve the cars they built. So education competition only works *if* it leads to school redesign, and there is scant evidence for that in education so far. What is important is school redesign, regardless of the competitive environment

Others argue that schools just need more money. But if that argument were valid, high-spending schools would be doing better than low-spending schools, and that's not always the case. Studies have found that even when resources increase substantially, schools frequently do not use the new dollars to strategically improve performance (Picus, Odden, Aportela, Mangan, & Goetz, 2008).

I am confident that school performance can improve even when funding is constrained. This conclusion draws from my work with my colleague Lawrence O. Picus on school finance adequacy (Odden & Picus, 2008), studies of schools and districts that have literally doubled student performance on state tests over a four- to six-year period (Odden, 2009; Odden & Archibald, 2009), and partnerships with districts in reallocating resources to more powerful education visions.

Indeed, the job of educators in a public system is always to keep focused on the main task—improving student performance and closing achievement gaps—regardless of the environment, whether that is changing student demographics or tight budgets. Boosting student learning when resources are rising admittedly is easier than doing so in times of tight—let alone falling—budgets. Especially in the fiscal context surrounding most school districts in 2011, this imperative—keeping the focus on student learning and aligning resources to that end—is critical as school budgets all around the country will do well to stay even, with many school budgets declining by hundreds of dollars per pupil in states like Florida and Texas. Thoughtlessly cutting positions in these contexts is not a wise strategy nor is saying that student performance will drop because budgets are dropping.

This chapter addresses what schools and district can do to retain the focus on student learning when funding is tight or even reduced. The main point of the chapter is that districts and schools must respond to these fiscal realities in strategic ways—to make sure that available resources are tightly aligned to an effective Plan of Action, with this book using the Plan of Action described in Chapter 1 as an example of how to make such alignments. The first section of this chapter argues that the first step is to understand and resist the cost increase pressures on schools. The second section provides an example of how one school—a middle school in the Midwest—could use its staffing resources more strategically and could even add new strategic elements if its budget were cut. The third section addresses a broader set of issues for how schools and districts could engage in strategic budgeting by reassessing the way they organize the instructional program, teacher work, and student schedules to ensure effectiveness and cost efficiency.

A key theme throughout this chapter is that educators—teachers and administrators—need to be flexible and not rigid about class sizes; rigidity about class sizes not only is very expensive but also limits the ability to deploy other needed strategies, thus likely having a negative impact on the bottom line—student achievement.

Understand and Resist the Cost Increase Pressures on Schools

Our current system of local control of education works well, but it tends to be more effective in boosting costs than student performance. Four key factors are behind these cost increase pressures.

Smaller Classes

Most districts find that reducing class size by one or two students eats up large portions of the budget and has generally modest impacts on achievement. To be sure, research (mainly the Tennessee STAR experiment) does support class-size reduction, but only for Grades K–3. In that study, larger classes (24–25 students) were compared to similar-size classes with an instructional aide as well as to smaller classes (15–17 students).

The findings were clear and undisputed. The small class sizes (but not the regular classes with an instructional aide) did positively impact student achievement (about 0.25 standard deviations) for all students (Nye, Hedges, & Konstantopoulos, 2002) and about twice that for students from low-income and minority (primarily African American) backgrounds (Krueger & Whitmore, 2001). So there was a positive impact; moreover, research shows that the positive impact continued on into middle and high school as well as in experiences beyond high school (Finn, Gerger, Achilles, & Zaharias, 2001; Krueger, 2002; Nye, Hedges, & Konstantopulos, 2001). Thus, according to the findings of this randomized trial experiment (the gold standard of research), smaller class sizes in the early grades do positively impact student performance in both the short and long term. But this evidence pertains only to Grades K–3 and only to class sizes of around 15 students and is smaller than the effects of other educational strategies discussed in this chapter. Unfortunately, there is no similar research on class-size reduction in upper elementary, middle, and high schools.

Yet pressure to reduce class size remains a high priority for many school districts. This causes a dilemma for most districts, because after the smaller classes are funded, there's little left to fund anything else. Indeed, a 2011 poll by *Education Next* (Howell, West, & Peterson, 2011) found the public wants taxes to stay flat or decline but also wants education spending to increase. And when asked to pick between two equally costly ways to spend more—higher teacher salaries ($10,000 per teacher) or lower class sizes (a reduction of three students)—the public chose smaller classes—the high-cost, small-impact/gain strategy.

More Electives

The public also pressures schools to offer many elective courses—art, music, health, and physical education; career and technical education; advanced classes such as Chinese 4 or Spanish 6; fun classes such as jewelry making or cheerleading; and so on. To respond, schools often expand to seven or eight periods a day, an option that increases costs by 20 to 40 percent compared to a six-period day. Further, because many elective classes are small and often taught by senior teachers, the cost per pupil can be four to five times the per-pupil spending on core courses (Roza, 2010).

There's little corresponding pressure—other than from parents of children with disabilities—to provide extra help for struggling students. These include programs such as extra tutoring, extended-day programming, English as a second language (ESL) instruction, and summer programs. Since parents of many of these students often don't have enough political clout to get these services, the calls for smaller classes and more electives often carry the day with local school boards.

Automatic Pay Increases

Nearly all school districts compensate teachers via step and lane salary schedules that produce virtually automatic annual pay increases. Even if the prices for everything else that a school district buys stays the same, districts need more money each year, because teachers and administrators have moved up a step of experience and/or across an education lane and are due those salary increases. If the entire salary schedule is increased for a cost-of-living adjustment, the impact of these automatic increases is even greater. This is a key reason why structural budget gaps exist every year, gaps that grow larger in states with more inelastic tax structures.

Since salary structures aren't linked to the twin strategic goals of improved teaching and higher achievement (Odden, 2008a), salary schedules not only push up costs but also have virtually no positive impact on system performance.

Growing Benefit Costs

Finally, the public is realizing that pension and health benefits are another huge draw on the education dollar. Moreover, few districts that provided retiree health benefits actually funded them, but accounting standards now require that they do so, and this money comes off the top of every year's budget. Further, most districts are experiencing large increases in health and pension costs for those still working (see Chapter 4 for further discussion of this issue).

Increased Costs and Flat Performance

In sum, schools are buffeted by intense pressures—smaller classes, more electives, automatic pay increases, and costly health and pension benefits—all of which increase costs and none of which have significant positive impacts on student learning. The public pressures school boards, school boards respond, and the system moves on each year with higher costs. No wonder spending per pupil has risen dra-matically in the past three decades while performance has been flat or only modestly increasing.

How to Move Forward

Recognizing these cost pressures is one thing; moving forward in a strategic manner is another. The book argues that to move forward in ways that strategically link resources to learning, schools and dis-tricts need

- clear goals
- a programmatic Plan of Action to achieve those goals
- clear understanding of the core resource needs of that Plan of Action
- engagement in strategic budgeting to align the resources they have to the resource needs of the Plan of Action
- a set of principles to guide such budget decisions

As Chapter 1 indicates, the book is based on the premise that the prime goals for all schools in America are to boost student learning in the core academic subjects—mathematics, science, history, reading/ English/language arts/writing, and foreign language—as well as thinking, problem solving, and communication in those content areas and reducing achievement gaps linked to demographics. Chapter 1 also detailed this book's Plan of Action for attaining those goals. Chapter 2 outlined in specific terms the resource needs of those strategies.

Chapter 2 also implied that there were three categories of schools vis-à-vis the resources needed to implement the book's Plan of Action: (1) those with more funds than the Plan requires, (2) those facing bud-get cuts, and (3) those with resources significantly less than the Plan.

The task for schools funded at or above these levels is to use those resources to attain the core student performance goals. But if those schools' current Plans of Action are not powerful enough to produce desired levels of learning, their task over a number of years is to understand and adopt the Plan of Action outlined in Chapter 1 and reallocate their staffing resources toward these strategies.

The task for schools with sufficient funding but facing budget reductions is to use the core programmatic and resource recommen-dations outlined in Chapters 1 and 2 to help determine what cuts will have the least impact on student performance—for example, slightly larger classes, fewer instructional aides, less focus on pullout reme-dial programs, and fewer administrators.

The task for schools with inadequate resources is to fund as much of the Plan of Action as possible, using six macro-strategies for allocating scarce dollars:

1. Use the staffing recommendations in Chapter 1's Plan of Action as a general guideline and reallocate current staff to these configurations.

2. Be flexible about class size.

3. Organize schools so that all key teacher groups have at least three 45-minute periods a week for collaborative work, even if it means increasing class sizes.

4. Do everything possible to make Tier 1 instruction—the core program—as effective as possible.

5. Provide all of the resources to help teachers and students—especially instructional coaches and staff for extra help strategies—by varying class size if necessary, allowing class size in secondary schools to rise substantially before reducing the instructional coach and extra help staff.

6. If increasing class size still does not allow the school to fund all the needed staff, then reductions in instructional coaching, extended-day programs and summer school, and lastly, tutoring staff should be considered.

These macro-principles for resource allocation have emerged from working sessions with faculty and administrators in the schools and districts all over the areas where I have worked. In those schools, small class size was not the driving consideration. Instead, such schools concluded that instructional coaches were necessary to improve core classroom instruction for all students and that time for teacher collaboration during the regular school day was also critical to improve core Tier 1 instruction, which is the foundation upon which all other strategies are built. They also argued that teacher/tutors were the most effective initial intervention strategy for struggling students, particularly for reading, so funding teacher/tutors as a Tier 2 strategy was a priority.

In sum, the overall Plan of Action and its particular staffing formulas and configurations can provide guidance for estimating an adequate level of education funding. They can serve as a structure for schools with higher levels of resources that are facing budget reductions and offer guidance to schools with less funding than needed for these staffing configurations as they face further cuts (or if, at some time in the future, they benefit from increases in revenue).

An Example of Strategic Resource Reallocation for a Midwestern Middle School

Table 3.1 shows the staffing and revenues in a Midwestern middle school a few years ago. It represents several aspects of many middle schools around the country. First, it has about 600 students, a modest size for a middle school but commensurate with the research on the most effective sizes for secondary schools (Lee & Smith, 1997). Second, the budget is over $4.3 million—a large amount. Indeed, principals of these modest-sized middle schools run multimillion-dollar organizations. Third, it has a large number of certified staff: 34 core and elective teachers, with the number of elective teachers close to half that of core teachers; 10.5 categorical program teachers for struggling students; 13.5 regular instructional aides; and a modest number (3.3) of student support staff (guidance counselors, nurses, social workers, etc.). It also has two assistant principals. Further, it has a seven-period schedule, with teachers providing instruction for just five of those periods. The seven-period schedule is one of the main reasons the school has so many elective teachers. But for a seven-period schedule, the school would need only 9.6 elective teachers; the reason it has more is that several of the elective classes have fewer students than do the regular classes (which have just under 25).

In short, the school has substantial resources—including a large number of staff—but many of them are not aligned with the staff requirements in Chapter 1's Plan of Action. It has no instructional coaches, and none of the categorical program teachers function in a teacher/tutor role (I know this from studying the school). And though there is a seven-period schedule, teachers do not use the extra plan period for collaborative work. So although it has many staff, they are not used in the best ways to promote greater student learning growth.

We could ask several questions about the staffing in this school: Could staff be deployed differently, more aligned with the staffing requirements of the Plan of Action formulas in Chapter 2? Could the school absorb budget cuts? If cuts were required of four or eight positions, what would be the most strategic ways to make those cuts? Could the school make such cuts and still continue to improve instructional practice and student learning? The next paragraphs ask and suggest answers to all of these questions.

Table 3.1   Current Revenues of a Midwestern Middle School (600 students; 50 percent poverty, 25 percent English language learners)

Title	Positions (FTE)	Revenue Per Position	Total Revenues
Principal	1	$100,000	$100,000
Assistant principals	2	$85,000	$170,000
Instructional support staff	0	$70,000	$0
Classroom teachers	23	$70,000	$1,610,000
Specialist teachers	11	$70,000	$770,000
Categorical program teachers for mild special education, compensatory education, ESL, gifted and talented students, etc.	10.5	$70,000	$735,000
Counselors	1	$70,000	$70,000
Other pupil support staff	3.2	$70,000	$224,000
Instructional aides	13.5	$20,000	$270,000
Supervisory aides	2.67	$17,500	$46,725
Librarians	1.3	$70,000	$91,000
Secretary/clerk	3	$30,000	$90,000
Discretionary Funds			
Professional development			$30,000
Equipment and technology			$50,000
Instructional materials			$84,000
Gifted and talented education			$15,000
Total of other discretionary funds			$0
Total Actual School Revenues			**$4,355,725**

ESL = English as a second language
FTE = full-time equivalent
Note: Table excludes all revenues for students with severe disabilities but includes revenues for such programs as desegregation, compensatory education (Title I or state), ESL and bilingual education, and the mild disabilities portion of state and federal handicapped funding.

The first question is, Could this school afford the staffing in Table 2.1—the full version of all the staffing required to dramatically improve student learning? The answer is yes, as Table 3.2 indicates.[2] Actually, Table 3.2 shows the school can afford, via staffing reallocation, everything in the Plan of Action—as well as the additional costs of the school's current seven-period a day schedule! Table 3.2 shows that it would require only $40,000 more to fully realign all of the school's resources to the staffing formulas for Chapter 1's Plan of Action (and a seven-period schedule). Table 3.2 shows that it would need about the same number of core teachers but fewer elective courses. It would require only ⅓ assistant principal but would allocate three full-time positions for instructional coaches, compared to two assistant principals and no instructional coaches in the existing school. If each instructional coach took on a version of the assistant principal position for Grades 6, 7, and 8, then the ⅓ assistant principal position arguably could be dropped, saving $28,000—close to what the school is short of fully funding the Plan of Action.

Table 3.2 shows that many staff positions can be reallocated to other, more specific purposes. First, a number of the excess elective positions can be reallocated to strategies for struggling students. Staff for such students would rise from 10.5 staff in Table 3.1 to 13.5 staff in Table 3.2—3 full-time equivalent (FTE) positions for teacher/tutors, 1.5 FTE teachers to provide ESL instruction to the school's students who do not speak English as their native language (25 percent of the student population), 2.5 positions each for extended-day and summer school programming, and four teacher and two aide positions to provide services for students with mild and moderate disabilities. This comprehensive set of staffing represents a large increase for a more sequenced, more integrated, and more focused set of services for struggling students than the hodgepodge of programs the school had provided with the previous 10.5 staff (who were mainly used for special education services). The Plan of Action would also include more student support staff, driven by the high poverty rate of the students in the school.

If the staffing allocations in Table 3.2 were used in the suggested ways, I would argue the school could double its student performance on state tests—with no extra money or staffing (Odden, 2009). That would clearly represent a huge productivity rise and significant reallocation of resources—something most educators claim is not possible in education, which is a labor-intensive activity. But as should be clear, it is the labor that gets reallocated and redeployed to actions and practices that simply have a much larger impact on student

Table 3.2 Costs of the Staffing Formulas for the Plan of Action (600 students; 50 percent poverty, 25 percent English language learners)

Elements of Model	Number of Positions Needed to Comply With the Plan of Action	Cost of Positions
Principals	1	$100,000
Assistant principals	0.33	$28,333
Instructional facilitators	3	$210,000
Classroom teachers	24	$1,680,000
Specialist teachers	9.6	$672,000
Teacher/tutors	3	$210,000
ELL/LEP teachers	1.5	$105,000
Extended-day teachers	2.5	$175,000
Summer school teachers	2.5	$175,000
Special education teachers (non-severe)	4	$280,000
Special education aides (non-severe)	2	$40,000
Counselors	2.4	$168,000
Other pupil support staff	3	$210,000
Supervisory aides	2.67	$53,333
Librarians	1.33	$93,333
Secretary/clerk	2.67	$80,000
Discretionary Funds		
Professional development		$60,000
Instructional materials		$84,000
Gifted and talented education		$15,000
Total Design Costs		**$4,370,600**

ELL/LEP = English language learners/Limited English proficiency learning. So far, we have shown how the school could reallocate its scarce resources (mostly staff) to produce large gains in student learning—something it might have argued it couldn't do without more dollars.

The above changes were possible a few years ago, before budget cuts. Suppose the school had to cut four FTE-certified positions. How could it respond? The answer is in many ways: (1) it could increase class size, (2) it could cut some of the staff providing extra help, (3) it could cut some of the student support staff (a category often cut first), or (4) it could cut instructional aides. It would have many choices.

Referring back to Table 3.1, it could cut some positions if it simply made all electives the same size as core classes—25 students. That would allow it to reduce its 11 elective positions to 9.6 positions, a modest pick-up of 1.4 positions. It would still need to cut 2.6 more positions, so it could cut the number of instructional aides; 3.5 positions would equal 1 FTE teacher position, so the school could cut about 9 instructional aide positions and be done. Of course, teachers probably would not want such cuts, as teachers usually advocate for instructional aides. The dilemma is that the same research that shows that small classes in kindergarten through Grade 3 improves student achievement also shows that students in a regular class with an instructional aide did no better than students in such classes without instructional aides (Finn & Achilles, 1999). So schools could cut instructional aides and have no negative impact on student learning.[3]

The school also could drop the seven-period schedule, which costs more than a six-period schedule. The typical middle school had a six-period schedule that included a range of electives years ago, before even more electives and an additional period were added to many middle schools. Dropping from a seven- to a six-period schedule would require 4.8 fewer elective teachers: more than a four FTE-position cut.

The point so far is that this school began with substantial resources and could easily absorb a four FTE-position cut—with virtually no impact on student achievement in the core subjects.

But the school has even more possibilities than just discussed. What if it wanted collaborative plan time for teachers and had to take a four FTE-position cut? We have seen such schools around the country decide to shift to a 90-minute block schedule and to raise class sizes. To address this task, let's work from Table 3.2 that shows a staffing situation (together with a seven-period day) that fully funds Chapter 1's Plan of Action and represents the initial capability to more effectively deploy this school's staff. The school could first cut four teaching positions (actually 4.8) by dropping to a six-period day (just for discussion and budgeting purposes) and use this as its most efficient core and elective teacher totals (29 FTE positions—24 core and 5 elective teachers). Then the school could adopt a 90-minute, four-block schedule with teachers teaching three blocks and elective teachers teaching the remaining blocks, giving teachers 45 minutes for individual plan time and 45 minutes for collaborative plan time, or 90 minutes of individual plan and collaborative time every other day. But to keep the costs of the block schedule the same as the six-period schedule (29 FTE positions—24 core and 5 elective teachers), class sizes would need to be raised to 28, which with the block schedule would require the same 29 teachers—22 core teachers and 7 elective teachers. Of course, the faculty would have to be willing to be flexible with their views toward class size *and* highly value teacher collaborative time. The school could retain the seven-period schedule (instead of the four-a-day, 90-minute block schedule) and require teachers to collaborate during the second pupil-free period, but that would be more costly than the block schedule approach or would require class sizes to rise to close to 30 to match the costs of the six-period schedule.

If the school needed to absorb even more cuts, its decisions would be more limited; however, I would argue that, as mentioned earlier, core and elective teachers together with teacher collaborative time should be retained, so the school should look to other parts of the staffing for cuts. I would also urge the school to retain the full number of instructional coaches, as coaches are key to strengthening the core (Tier 1) instructional program and helping teachers engage in data-based decision making. Four more cuts would require the school to assess the student support staff and the set of services for struggling students, a set of resources now available to very few schools. I would probably advise the school to retain the teacher/tutor staff until the bitter end (because research shows that teacher/tutors have large impacts on student-learning gains) and cut the extended-day staff first, as the research is quite mixed about the impact of extended-day programs (mainly due to poor implementation and low attendance).

So the point of this one-school example is that it has many options for improving performance without any new money, and even for improving student learning if it had to make budget cuts—initially cutting four staff positions and then eight positions. If it retains a Plan of Action like that discussed in Chapter 1, it can still tightly align resources to strategies that improve student learning while also cutting staff—with eight staff positions representing significant cuts.

Though no budget cut is wanted, no school should despair if one is needed. If it has appropriate goals—higher levels of student performance in core subjects (like the schools and districts referenced in Chapter 1)—has a research- and best-practice-based Plan of Action (or education improvement strategy or whatever it wants to call its strategy to boost performance), and knows how to align staffing resources to the elements of that Plan of Action *and is not rigid about class size*, it should be able to act in a nimble and effective manner in today's tight fiscal times.

More Detail on Strategic Budgeting

While collaborating with Lawrence O. Picus and Associates, I worked with several districts around the country in a strategic budget alignment process, which seeks to align whatever resources schools have to strategies most likely to boost performance. This section of the chapter discusses in more detail many of the issues of more effective resource use that have emerged from this work at the local level, including variations in class size—which sometimes involves raising class sizes to produce staffing slots that can be used for other highly valued programmatic efforts, such as teacher/tutors for struggling students and instructional coaches for teachers. This section also discusses more detail around elective versus core classes, finding time for collaborative teacher work, the costs of professional development, and identifying and resourcing a sequence of integrated actions focused on helping struggling students achieve proficiency (if not advanced performance).

Class Size

Decisions about class size compose the largest draw on any education budget. It turns out that class sizes ranged all over the board in the schools and districts dramatically improving performance—several years ago, some reduced class size to 15 in Grades K–3, but others did not, and many of the urban schools in various studies had class sizes from the mid-20s up to the 30s. So it could be argued the class size may or may not be a key element of strategies to turn around low-performing schools or to boost performance in high-performing schools. These finding suggest class size decisions can be quite elastic—and even the last to fund when dollars are scarce. And as the following discussion shows, this flexible perspective on class size is shared by most of the districts with which we have worked.

Nevertheless, when initially asked to outline their education improvement strategy, most teachers and administrators identify smaller class sizes as the lead element. That is both an expensive approach and (because of its draw on budget resources) nearly always reduces what can be spent on the other elements of Chapter 1's Plan of Action, thus dramatically reducing the impact of the overall strategy. After discussion and analysis, though, many schools and districts with which we work decide to abandon their quest for smaller and smaller class sizes in order to fund more of the elements of a comprehensive overall education improvement strategy.

However, because class size is the largest staffing element, the starting point for budget decisions must be class size, and the most effective class sizes should be culled from the research literature. Unfortunately, as discussed previously, there is only significant research on class size reduction for Grades K–3. This research showed that smaller class sizes in the early grades do positively impact student performance in the short, medium, and long term. But this evidence pertains only to Grades K–3 and only to class sizes around 15. Unfortunately, there is no similar research on class size reduction in upper elementary, middle, and high school grades.

Thus, as presented in Chapter 2, our adequacy reports recommend core class sizes of 15 students in Grades K–3 and 25 students in subsequent grades, the latter being about the national median. For an average-sized elementary school—400 to 500 students—these class size recommendations average 18 students across Grades K–5 in the typical elementary school. Research would not support a policy of, for example, setting class sizes at 20 for elementary schools or reducing class size from 25 to 22, even though such initiatives emerge all over the country—sometimes in state and even federal policy.

The Tennessee experiment also found that putting an instructional aide in a regular class had no impact on student learning! Thus, the policy and practice around the country of adding instructional aides to classrooms to reduce the student-adult ratios are ineffective uses of resources. Some states mandate this practice for all Grades K–3; other districts add instructional aides when class sizes exceed a certain number, often setting that number in the high teens. Again, these are ineffective uses of resources. Thus, all schools that have instructional aides in regular classrooms should reassess the practice, because the research that exists shows the practice has no positive impact on student learning.

As stated above, these class size recommendations are starting points *if* the budget can support them and, I would add at this point, *if* all the other elements of the Plan of Action are fully funded. In other words, because of the importance and larger impacts of the other programmatic aspects of the Plan of Action, *small classes should be the last to be implemented,* not the first.

All this information suggests that the recommended class size numbers are not sacrosanct. In working with several districts on how to restructure their budgets to more strategically align them with improvement strategies, we found the following:

- One suburban district in the Northwest, with rising numbers and percentages of students from lower-income and non-English-speaking backgrounds, identified finding collaborative time for teachers as a prime objective. Their middle schools and high schools decided to raise class size into the low- to mid-30s in order to have a block schedule that provided teachers with 45 minutes a day for collaborative team work and 45 minutes a day for individual teacher plan time.

- An urban district in the Midwest staffed its 32 K–8 schools by grade level with the goal of having class sizes of 18. But, if the pupil count was not an exact multiple of 18, a teacher plus an instructional aide was provided for class sizes from 19 to 26. If the class size exceeded 26, that student group would be split into two classes to produce class sizes of 13+. This approach produced several cliff effects, where one additional student required adding either an aide or a teacher position, totaling a considerable numbers of additional teachers and instructional aides. By staffing at an average of 25 students in a class, the district could have saved about 400 instructional aide positions and nearly 60 teacher positions.

- An analysis in Ohio (Partin, 2010) showed the following points:
  ○ If every district in the Buckeye State raised its average student-teacher ratio by one student (for example, from 16-to-1 to 17-to-1), there was a potential savings of $276 million in teachers' salaries alone.
  ○ If the districts with ratios lower than 20-to-1 raised their ratios to that level, the state could save $458 million in teachers' salaries.
  ○ If the districts with ratios lower than 22-to-1 raised their ratios to that level, the state could save $848 million in teachers' salaries.
  ○ If every Ohio district operated at an average 25-to-1 student-teacher ratio, the state could save $1.38 billion in teachers' salaries alone.

Though this analysis confused student-teacher ratios with class size,[4] the data nevertheless demonstrate how small increases in class size can produce millions of dollars of unallocated resources, something all districts should consider when budgets are tight.

- As another example, take a district with 2,500 students—close in size to the median district in the country. Suppose it had been staffing its schools with an average of 24 students in a class. Assuming six-period days with teachers providing instruction for five periods, that class size approach would have required about 100 teachers, assuming all classes were of equal size. Shifting the class size to 26 would reduce the call for teachers to 96—a savings of four positions—with little impact on student performance. Hiking class sizes to 27 would produce position savings of about eight positions.

- Most districts believe that Advanced Placement (AP) classes should be no larger than 15 students. There is really no performance rationale for that low number. AP classes could be raised to 25 or even 30 students without a loss in student performance; such changes could allow a district to significantly expand the number of students in AP classes at no additional cost (except for the training costs, which would be subsumed under the professional development budget recommended below) or have teacher positions freed up for other purposes. One Midwest suburban district decided to increase AP classes from 15 to 25 students to produce several teaching positions that the district wanted to use for expanding their extra help services for struggling students, representing a shift from spending more on the brightest high-achievers to spending more on the struggling student (while still providing the high-achievers with their advanced classes).

Class size decisions are critical. Districts and schools can start with some number—perhaps the recommended figures from adequacy studies—but all educators should know that they can be flexible in setting class sizes with little (if any) impact on student performance. Educators also need to know that research supports small class sizes only in the early elementary grades and that the costs of that more-targeted policy are high and the benefits modest.

Willing to be flexible about class sizes could be one of the most important aspects of aligning resources with student learning in these times of tight education budgets. The culture in America's schools—as well as public pressure—so strongly supports small class size that raising class size is often the last practice to change when money becomes scarce, and then only after severe cuts to all other programs and services. The book argues that districts and schools should take the exact opposite perspective—consider raising class sizes as the first budget initiative in tight fiscal times. Not only will modest hikes in class size not negatively impact student learning, but also it will provide the system with the more fiscal flexibility to maintain other, more effective programs

School Schedules and Core Versus Elective Teachers

Second to class size, the mix of core and elective classes is the next largest draw on the education dollar. Electives have expanded substantially in America's schools. Course offerings data show that in American high schools, the number of elective classes often exceeds the number of core classes.

With accountability focused so much on student performance in core subjects, one might expect that spending per pupil on core subjects would exceed that of elective classes. But detailed research shows otherwise. In studies of multiple high schools, Roza (2010) found that expenditures per pupil for most elective classes exceeded that for core courses! She found cheerleading classes at one high school cost $36,000 per pupil and jewelry making cost $20,000 per pupil, compared with costs of $5,000 to $7,000 per pupil for classes such as algebra and biology. This represents a major misallocation of the education dollar—certainly not a use of resources that is aligned with the core goals of the education system.

Roza's study also showed that the two reasons for the high costs of some electives were small numbers of students in most of them and the use of the most senior teachers to provide instruction in them. The combination of more elective classes, small elective class sizes, and more-expensive teachers teaching them produced the imbalance of resource allocation—more to electives and less to core subjects. In many districts and schools, neither teachers nor administrators are aware of these practices and their resultant budget realities.

I repeat a principle made earlier: all children should have access to a liberal arts education in all grades. Thus, schools need to have an array of electives as well as core classes. But offering more and spending more on electives than on core classes is antithetical to the goal of improved student performance in the core subjects. Thus, every district, and especially every secondary school and every high school, should analyze spending by class; if the results parallel those of Roza's study, changes should be in order.

School Schedules. Elective expenditures and costs are closely linked to school schedules. Over the past two to three decades, many middle and high schools have adopted seven- and eight-period schedules. One factor behind these shifts was the middle school model that included more elective options for students and a seven-period day; demand for more and more electives primarily drove the period expansions in high schools. These shifts accommodated provision of more courses for students, but since teaching loads remained constant, they increased the overall cost—and reduced the number of minutes of instruction in all subjects, including core subjects—as shown in Table 3.3.

Decades ago, most middle and high schools had six-period days (usually 55 minutes of instruction with 5 minutes for students to change classrooms), and teachers would teach five of those periods, leaving one period for individual planning and preparation. Under this structure, a school needed 1.2 teachers to cover the six periods and maintain the student-teacher ratio under which teachers were allocated to schools. When schools shifted to a seven-period schedule and teachers maintained a five-class teaching load, the school needed 1.4 teachers for the same class size. Schools that implemented eight-period schedules and maintained the five-period teaching load needed 1.6 teachers to maintain class sizes—1 teacher for the five periods and 0.6 teacher for the additional three periods.

Since schools rarely extended the school day as the number of periods increased, the number of minutes for each class period was also reduced from 55 minutes to 46 minutes to 40 minutes. A seven-period day thus increases elective offerings, but also results in greater costs and fewer minutes of instruction in all classes, including core

Table 3.3 Staffing Needs and Instructional Time With Different Schedules

Number of Periods	Numbers of Teachers Needed for Every Five Class Periods*	Length of the Instructional Period**
6	1.2	55
7	1.4	46
8	1.6	40

*Assuming teachers instruct for five periods daily

** In minutes, assuming five minutes of passing time between periods and a 6.5-hour day subjects. An eight-period day costs even more and further reduces instructional minutes. These impacts of more-expanded schedules detract substantially from the goal of improving student achievement in core subjects. And there is no research showing that schools with seven- and eight-period schedules produce more student learning gains than does the six-period schedule, including research on the middle school model.

In these times of fiscal shortfall and continuing increased emphasis on student learning in core subjects, districts would be wise to rethink seven- and eight-period schedules in their secondary schools. For example, a middle school of 1,000 students with average class sizes of 25 students would need 40 core teachers and another 8 more teachers for electives (20 percent of the number of core teachers) if it had a six-period schedule. But it would need a total of 16 elective teachers if it had a seven-period schedule. Thus, if the school shifted from a seven- to a six-period schedule, it would free up eight teaching positions, some of which could be used to solve a fiscal shortage and some of which could be used both to provide teachers with instructional coaches and struggling students with small-group tutoring—two high-cost strategies that are associated with large improvements in student learning. Several middle schools in a Midwest district have already implemented a shift back to a six-period schedule, saving dozens of teacher positions.

Career-Technical Programs. Another major issue concerning electives, course offerings, and the school schedule is the nature of programs designed to provide skills for specific careers after high school. Decades ago, the dominant programs were home economics; business and shorthand; wood, plastic, auto, and metal shop; mechanical drawing; welding; agricultural economics, and so on. Today, largely driven by changes in the economy that require all students to be college-ready whether entering the workforce immediately after high school or enrolling in some type of postsecondary education experience (technical or four-year college), significant changes are being made in career-technical education (CTE) programs. New programs are focused on job areas that are expanding in today's economy—health professions, biotechnology, technology, computer-based manufacturing, and so on. Further, many of the courses—engineering, computer-aided design, biotechnology, DNA and forensics science, and so on—are legitimate substitutes for more traditional academic math and science courses.

One key issue is the cost of these programs. Many districts and states believe that these new career-technical programs cost more. But in a review conducted for a school finance adequacy task force, a national expert (Phelps, 2006) concluded that the best of the new career-technical programs did not cost more, especially if the district and state made adequate provisions for professional development (as teachers in these new programs needed training) and computer technologies (as computer technologies were heavily used). These conclusions were confirmed by a cost analysis (Odden & Picus, 2010) of Project Lead the Way (PLTW), one of the most highly rated and expensive career technical programs in the country.

PLTW (www.pltw.org) is a nationally prominent exemplar for secondary CTE education. These programs are often implemented jointly with local postsecondary education institutions and employer advisory groups and usually feature project- or problem-based learning experiences, career-planning and guidance services, and technical and/or academic skill assessments. The program is designed to develop the science, technology, engineering, and mathematics skills essential for achievement in the classroom and success in college or entry directly into the workforce through hands-on experience that prepares students for the real world. Developed in upstate New York schools in the early 1990s, PLTW is offered in more than 3,000 high schools in all 50 states and now enrolls over 350,000 total students.

The curriculum features rigorous, in-depth learning experiences delivered by certified teachers and end-of-course assessments. High-scoring students earn college credit recognized in more than 100 affiliated postsecondary institutions. Courses focusing on engineering foundations (design, principles, and digital electronics) and specializations (e.g., architectural and civil engineering or biotechnical engineering) provide students with career and college readiness competencies in engineering and science. Students need to take math up to Algebra 2 in order to handle the courses in the program, which also meets many state standards for science and other mathematics classes.

The major cost areas for the program are in class size, professional development, and computer technologies. Most programs recommend class sizes of 25 students, which is around the median for the country, and the professional development and most of the computer technologies would be covered by the professional development and computer allocations discussed in Chapter 2. Some of the PLTW concentration areas require the onetime purchase of some expensive equipment, which could be covered by around $9,000 per career-technical education teacher. The point: even the best, most effective, and highest-cost career-technical programs are not costly.

Summary. In these tight fiscal times, all districts and schools need to reassess schedules in middle schools and high schools, the plethora of elective courses being offered, and the viability of replacing older vocational education programs with newer career-technical programs. Every school—including elementary schools—should provide a liberal arts education to all students. But enhancing that approach and adding electives and increasing costs by having seven- and eight-period schedules is antithetical to the goals of increasing student performance in core subjects and allocating resources first to strategies and structures that help attain those goals.

Since the public generally pressures schools for smaller classes as well as more electives, school leaders cannot make the programmatic changes and fiscal efficiencies discussed so far without support from the broader political body and the general public. This means that districts and schools need to inform the public—especially parents—about how school resources are now spent and why, in these tight fiscal times, they are proposing to modestly hike class sizes as well as rein in the number of electives. And political leaders outside of education should be encouraged to support these brave moves.

Put differently, there is a substantive and political issue involved in the budgeting issues surrounding class size and electives; educators will not be able to make the changes previously proposed unless political leaders outside of education—and over time, the public and parents—support such changes.

Professional Development

Every study of improving schools and districts identifies intensive, long-term, and ongoing professional development as a critical ingredient. Few, however, specifically identify the resources needed for such programs, though the presence of instructional coaches is a relatively new and constant ingredient all over the country. After reviewing the research on the features of effective professional development, Odden and Picus (2008) concluded that the following resources are needed to deploy effective, intensive professional development, which is key to transforming all the resources from the Plan of Action into effective instructional practices that boost student learning:

1. Time during the summer for intensive training institutes. This training can most easily be accomplished by ensuring that approximately 10 days of the teacher's normal work year are dedicated to professional development. Thus, the teacher's work year needs to include at least 10 pupil-free days for such training—and districts should keep primary control over the use of these days for systemic training on the district's and schools' approach to curriculum and instructional change. These are days in addition to the approximate 180 days of instructing students, days for opening and closing school, and parent-teacher conference days.

For an average teacher salary ($50,000) plus benefits (40 percent of salary, which totals about $70,000), and 200 typical workdays, this costs $350 a day or $3,500 for the 10 days. Since most teachers already have some professional development days, we have found that states generally need to add about 5 days to the typical teacher work year to total 10 pupil-free days, so the incremental costs is often half of $3,500.

2. On-site coaching for all teachers to help them incorporate new instructional practices into their instructional repertoire. The basic recommendation is at least one instructional coach for every school (assuming about 500 students in the school, so two coach positions for a school with 1,000 students), increasing the numbers of instructional coaches—if resources allow—to one instructional coach for every 200 students.

Instructional coaches are generally paid on the teacher salary schedule. So if teachers average 25 students in their class, each teacher triggers ⅛ of an instructional coach, or $8,750 per teacher ($70,000/8).

3. Collaborative work with teachers in their schools during planning and preparation periods to improve the curriculum and instructional program, thus reinforcing the strategic and instrumental need for planning and preparation time during the regular school day, which can be provided if school staffing includes elective teachers. This requires smart scheduling of teachers during the regular school day and week and is discussed below.

However, as discussed above, we code elective teachers as elective and *not* professional development costs. But, *if* this was coded as a professional development cost, it would equal 20 percent of the average teacher salary and benefits, or $14,000 per elementary or middle school teacher, and 33 percent for high school teachers, or $23,100 per teacher.

4. Funds for training during the summer and for ongoing training during the school year, the cost of which is about $50,000 for a school unit of 500 students or approximately $100/pupil, which is meant to cover any central office professional development staff as well as any outside consultants.

In sum, assuming an average teacher salary and benefits totals about $70,000, the specific costs of professional development over and above staffing for schools generally are

a. $3,500 per teacher for training time

b. $8,750 per teacher for instructional coaches/mentors/instructional facilitators

c. $100 per pupil for trainers and other administrative and miscellaneous costs. If each teacher averages 25 students, this cost item then is $2,500 per teacher.

These *costs total $14,750 per teacher,* or an extra 21 percent over a core teacher's salary and benefits.

Finally, if we converted the above per-teacher figures (excluding the elective teachers) to a per-pupil figure (assuming 25 students in each classroom), the costs of professional development would be $590 per pupil ($14,750/25). This figure for the *cost of professional development equals about 5.4 percent of an operating spending-per-pupil* figure of $11,000, which is close to the national average. This is a reasonable figure and represents a robust and comprehensive approach to funding all the requirements for an intensive, ongoing, and systemic professional development program that would address all school training needs over time.

Before assuming that this kind of professional development requires more funding, all districts should conduct a fiscal audit of existing professional development programs. Studies (e.g., Miles, Odden, Fermanich, & Archibald, 2004) have shown that urban districts already spend from $4,000 to $8,000 per teacher on existing professional development programs, too often with little focus on training in teaching core subjects. For these districts, professional development resources and programs need to be strategically realigned and targeted to curriculum and instructional efforts focused on core content areas and the specific, effective instructional vision being developed by the district and school.

In my first book on resource reallocation (Odden & Archibald, 2001), we found many schools that free up teacher resources through various resource reallocation efforts targeted professional development—mainly the provision of instructional coaches—as a prime target for the reallocated staff:

- Ambitious resource reallocation to fund comprehensive professional development programs was the foundation of the effective program in New York City's District #2 (Elmore & Burney, 1999), led by then-superintendent Anthony Alvarado. Alvarado and his central office staff dramatically expanded professional development by eliminating most of the categorical program and instructional support staff in the central office and turning the funds supporting those positions into dollars for professional development (see Elmore & Burney, 1999). The district eliminated nearly all district-level categorical program support staff for federal (Title I) and state compensatory education and bilingual education and reduced the amount of money used for special education program support. It took those funds and reallocated them to professional development—instructional coaches, summer institutes, and trainers—focused on reading, writing, and mathematics. Over a five-year period, the district expanded professional development expenditures to about 5 percent of its operating budget. It then used those funds to focus relentlessly on developing teachers' instructional expertise in reading. After that time period, the district's students produced one of the highest-ever scores on the New Standards Reference assessments.

- In my earliest resource reallocation research (Odden & Archibald, 2001), we found many schools that redeployed teachers from certain roles to instructional coach roles. Many schools have moved Title I reading teachers into instructional coach roles, working individually with classroom teachers to help them incorporate new instructional strategies, usually for reading and mathematics, into their ongoing repertoire. We also found many elementary schools traded their certified library position for an instructional coach position, putting an aide in the library and automating the circulation system for library books.

- A rural district in the Northwest with high concentrations of English language learner (ELL) students that also doubled its student performance in reading made budgetary decisions that identified professional development as a high priority by reallocating resources. That district cut back on maintenance, food service, and secretarial staffing to fund ongoing professional development at a high level.

- Over the past decade and a half, many schools that adopted the Success for All reading program reallocated remedial teacher and instructional aide positions that had been funded with federal Title I dollars for instructional coaches, outside training provided by the Success for All Foundation, and teacher/tutors who provided individual help to struggling students.

In short, schools that seriously moved the student achievement needle placed a high priority on intensive professional development and reallocated teacher positions, library positions, instructional aide positions, and small sums from other activities to bolster professional development so there could be summer institutes, ongoing training, and instructional coaches in all schools. They found that professional development was critical to making their Tier 1 core instructional program (often with a focus on reading) more effective and made funding its key elements a top priority.

As noted in Chapter 1, instructional coaches are important to this mix of professional development resources. Not only have all schools and districts that have moved the student achievement needle by large amounts provided for substantial numbers of instructional coaches, but there also is mounting research evidence that instructional coaching works. The most recent study, using a randomized trial approach, found that coaching secondary school teachers with a specific coaching approach—called MyTeaching Partner Secondary— produced significant, positive impacts on those teachers' ability to produce gains in student achievement in four academic subjects: mathematics, science, history, and language arts (Carlson et al., 2011). So instructional coaches or facilitators are key elements of effective professional development (see also, Crow, 2011).

Finding collaborative time. As discussed in Chapter 1, time for teachers to work in collaborative groups on curriculum and instructional issues is a recent addition to the set strategies schools deploy to boost student learning and is emerging consistently as a strategy in nearly all recent studies of schools moving the student achievement needle (Blankstein, 2010; DuFour, DuFour, & Eaker, 2008; DuFour, DuFour, Eaker, & Karhanek, 2010; Odden, 2009). The challenge is to find this time during the regular 6.5-hour school day.

Initially, teachers are reluctant to give up individual plan time, as they view the collaborative work as something different that adds to their workload. Over time, teachers often come to realize that the collaborative work actually replaces the need for many individual planning activities—and is much more effective—and become willing to substitute some individual plan time for collaborative work. To start the process of teachers collaborating, though, the challenge for most schools is finding collaborative plan time over and above individual plan time. In many charter schools, this is attained simply by having a school day that is 45–60 minutes longer than the typical 6.5-hour public school day, with the added time used for collaborative work or other professional development.

Without extending the school day, though, finding blocks of time for collaborative time for middle and high schools can be relatively straightforward: It can be found by increasing class size by 2–3 students (with the starting point at 25 students in a class) and shifting to four 90-minute blocks per day (a schedule that can accommodate 90-minute full-block periods as well as 45-minute skinny-block periods). Teachers would provide instruction for three of the blocks and have pupil-free time for the other block; this approach requires staffing schools at 1.33 teachers for each of four blocks (as compared to the 1.2 teachers for a six-period day). Both approaches (the six-period day or the four 90-minute block day) require 24 teacher positions (with 25 students in a class for the six-period approach and 27–28 students for the four-block approach) in a 500-student school, so neither has a cost advantage. Several districts with which we worked, however, not only began a strategic budget process of more tightly aligning their resources with strategies to boost learning with larger class sizes but were also still willing to raise them by a few students to attain the desired time for collaborative teacher work.

Providing time for collaborative work while retaining the individual planning time seems to be more difficult for elementary school teachers but can be accomplished. Elementary schools can organize a 6.5-hour school day into six 55-minute instructional blocks (which consumes 5.5 hours), two 15-minute recess periods or one 30-minute recess period (with aides covering recess so this time can be used for individual teacher planning), and a 30-minute lunch period. Teachers would provide instruction for five of the six instructional periods, leaving one pupil-free instructional block (the time when grade-level students would take electives, with the specific elective class taken— art, music, physical education, etc.—varying each day). Two of those five pupil-free periods could be used for individual planning time; when added to the planning time during recess, the total would provide the generally required five periods a week for individual planning. Three of the pupil-free periods during student elective time, then, could be used for collaborative team work by grade-level teachers. This approach can be accomplished with specified regular class sizes (whatever sizes can be afforded).

We found that even more time might be found for collaboration in elementary schools that enroll significant numbers of students needing extra help services. As an example, one school had 50 percent ELL students, who were pulled out of an instructional block and organized into appropriate groups for ESL instruction. The classes of the remaining students were thus half the regular size! By combining these classes (two half-size classes into one full-size class), faculties in some schools found that they could provide additional pupil-free periods for teachers (every other day, assuming the 50 percent concentration and heterogeneous classes). This approach freed up more of the common pupil-free time when students attended electives for more collaborative teacher work.

In sum, there are multiple ways schools and districts can restructure the hours in the regular school day and week to provide both sufficient individual plan time and sufficient (at least three 45- to 55-minute periods a week) collaborative team time without increasing staffing needs or school costs—and without days of early release of students. Of course, it often is the case that in the same district, some school schedules are organized to provide such time, while others are not so organized. So if collaborative time is desired—which it should be, as it is a key part of the overall Plan of Action—district leaders need to train principals in how to organize the school day to provide that time and insist that they do so.

Using collaborative time well. During the discussions in various districts on the search for teacher collaborative time, all districts made the point—multiple times—that their education systems needed to provide training to principals, teachers, and lead teachers (instructional coaches) in how to make good use of collaborative time. Each district recognized that time for teaches to work in collaborative teams was just the first step in having collaborative activities contribute to improved instruction and student learning. Principals would need to organize school schedules so all team members had free time at the same time during the day. Lead teachers and team coordinators need expertise in setting agendas, running meetings, keeping team members focused on the agenda, and helping diverse people make decisions; teachers need training in how to work effectively in collaborative groups. The consensus was the need to put in systems and considerable training, to ensure that all collaborative time was used well and that the potential of this new resource was realized.

Final comment. Readers should continue to note the flexibility schools and districts took with class sizes. In nearly every district and school that addressed strategic budgeting in the past several years, there was willingness on the part of teachers and principals to adjust class size to provide other highly valued resources—such as collaborative time, instructional coaches, and teacher/tutors—on the belief that these other resources more strongly impact student achievement in core subjects and that modest hikes in class size would not negatively impact that objective.

Extra Help Programs for Struggling Students

As noted in Chapter 1, effective schools and districts hold performance standards constant for students and expand instructional time, thus providing extra help to slower learners struggling to achieve to at least high proficiency—if not advanced—performance standards. Odden and Picus (2008) review a wide variety of research on such effective extra help strategies and conclude by recommending the following:

- *Teacher/tutors for Tier 2 intervention* assistance during the regular school day. The suggested formula is one teacher/tutor position for every 200 at-risk students, usually measured by the number of students from poverty backgrounds (determined by the number of students receiving free and reduced-price lunch), with a minimum of one position for every school of approximately 500 students. One-to-one tutoring is recommended for students in the bottom third of achievement; tutoring groups could rise to a maximum of five students struggling with less severe learning problems. This recommendation is sufficient to provide all the Tier 2 intervention that should be part of effective reading programs, as discussed in Chapter 1. Further, it could be appropriate to transform one teacher/tutor position into two trained instructional aide/tutor positions for students with milder learning challenges, but instructional aides should not be used to tutor students with more complex learning issues in the bottom half of achievement.
- *Staff for extended-day academic help* at the rate of 0.25 teacher positions for every 30 students at risk of academic failure (again, generally indicated by students eligible for free and reduced-price lunch). The programmatic recommendation is for class sizes of 15 students, with the assumption that only half of eligible students would actually attend such extended-day programming, and two hours of programming each day (thus about ¼ of the school day).

- *Staff for summer school programming* for a full 8-week (or so) summer session of six hours each day, with the bulk of instruction focused on academics. The suggested formula is a rate of 0.25 teacher positions for every 30 students at risk of academic failure (again, generally measured by students eligible for free and reduced-price lunch). The programmatic recommendation is for class sizes of 15 students, with the assumption that only half of eligible students would actually attend such summer school academic-focused programming, and with summer session running for about an extra quarter of the school year (thus the ¼ teacher position).

As the research reviews indicate (Odden & Picus, 2008), the impacts of individual and small-group tutoring are extremely high (over one standard deviation) and should garner high priority in the allocation of scarce resources. On the other hand, the impacts of extended-day and summer school programs vary substantially, mainly because of widely varying program structure and implementation. Good ones have high impacts; others do not (see also Borman & Boulay, 2004; Fashola, 1998; McCombs et al., 2011). Thus, the highest-priority resources should be given to the individual and small-group tutoring, then summer school, and then extended-day programs; but to be effective, the latter two must have a strong academic focus.

The framework for all these services, again, is Response to Intervention (RTI). Without getting into a formal definition of RTI, the concept is that students—all students—first need the highest-quality and most effective Tier 1 instruction in all core subjects, including some accommodations within the regular class. This is followed by Tier 2 instruction—a variety of interventions to extend instructional time and help all students stay on track to academic proficiency. These interventions include some combination of individual tutoring, small-group tutoring (not to exceed five students per group), and extended-day and summer school academic services. Special education, or Tier 3 instruction, then is provided but only *after* the appropriate provision of both Tier 1 and Tier 2 instruction. It also should be noted that this approach significantly reduces the need to give a student a label as a student with a disability and place them into a special education program (see, for example, Levenson, 2011; Madden, Slavin, Karweit, Dolan, & Wasik, 1993; Slavin, 1996).

In this vein, Odden and Picus (2008; www.lpicus.com) in both their school finance text and adequacy studies recommend that states resource special education services on what is called a census basis, which means providing resources for students needing special education services but for the same percentage of students in every district. This recommendation is accompanied by an additional recommendation for the state to fully fund services for the high-cost programs needed for students with severe and profound disabilities, the incidence of which is not evenly distributed across districts. Both of these strategies are made feasible only if there are resources for the full set of extra help programs described above. But this approach does change what has happened over the years—rising numbers of students have been identified as needing special education services, but many of them are simply students achieving below proficiency standards who have not received the kinds of Tier 2 interventions they need, which would have kept them on a path to proficient achievement.

Schools and districts took many paths to finding the resources for individual and small-group tutoring, summer school, and extended-day programming:

- Many schools around the country have transformed Title I reading teachers or Title I-supported resource room teachers into teacher/tutors who work with students in groups of one to five students.
- Many other schools and districts have eliminated or reduced instructional aides supported by categorical funds, including instructional aide funds for students with disabilities, and used the savings for a combination of teacher/tutors, extended-day programming, and summer school.
- Rosalia, a rural district in Washington with high concentrations of children from lower income and ELL backgrounds, simply reduced funding for its middle and high schools to provide for tutors in Grades K–3; Montgomery County in Maryland, a large urban district with increasing numbers of students from lower-income backgrounds and non-English-speaking families, did the same (Childress et al., 2009).
- Kennewick, Washington, used all teachers to provide instruction for a 120-minute literacy block each day and used trained instructional aides to provide reading instruction in middle schools while placing their teachers with most experience in teaching reading with the lowest-performing students in classes of four to five students for one hour of this instructional block.
- Other districts and schools have increased class sizes modestly to produce 1–2 teacher positions that they then used as

teacher/tutors for the lowest-performing and most-struggling students (Odden & Archibald, 2001).

- Many secondary schools—middle and high schools—organized double math or reading programs for struggling students, deciding that achieving proficiency in literacy and numeracy took precedence over some elective courses.

- There are fewer examples of schools reallocating resources to provide for extended-day or summer school programming. Usually, these programs received grant funding, sometimes from the federal Title I program but often from specific programs for extended-day or summer school programs. In part because these two strategies have mixed results on their effectiveness (due largely to high and low fidelity of program implementation), they have struggled to garner ongoing funding.

In sum, schools and districts took multiple paths toward resourcing these extra help strategies for students struggling to achieve to standards. Education systems in Wyoming and Arkansas, states where we have helped provide adequate school funding, have resources for these initiatives from ongoing state funding; other states would be wise to follow that strategy. Students struggling to meet rigorous standards, especially the emerging common core standards in reading and math, will need extra instructional time to achieve to those levels, and that extra time must be funded somehow.

Interim Assessments

Interim assessments—formative or short cycle, and benchmark—are instruments designed to provide detailed and concrete information on what students know and do not know with respect to discrete curriculum units and, over time, the interventions they need. When teachers have this information, they are able to design instructional activities that are more precisely tailored to the exact learning status of the students in their own classrooms and school. In this way, their instruction can be, to use a term from the business community, much more *efficient*: They know the goals and objectives they want students to learn, they know exactly what their students do and do not know with respect to those goals and objectives, and so they craft instructional activities and interventions specifically designed to help the students in their classrooms learn the goals and objectives for the particular curriculum unit.

Though state tests provide faculties with a big picture, or *macro-map*, of where the school has been effective and where it had been ineffective in producing student learning, interim assessments are needed to provide a micro-map for how teachers need to teach specific curriculum units, including appropriate interventions for struggling students. Interim assessment data provide teachers the additional, micro-level formative assessment and other screening data to design the details of daily lesson plans and interventions for curriculum units that are more effective in getting all students to learn the main objectives of the unit to proficiency. In sum, interim assessments are new but rapidly evolving educational tools (see Boudett, City, & Murnane, 2007; Boudett & Steele, 2007; Educational Leadership, 2007/2008). A recent randomized trial experiment showed that data-based decision making with some sort of interim assessments worked to boost student learning (see Carlson et al., 2011).

There are many sources for and types of interim assessments. One type, called MAP (Measures of Academic Progress), is used by many of the schools and districts we have studied and is available from the Northwest Evaluation Association (NWEA; www.nwea.org) in Portland, Oregon. These benchmark assessments are available online for a fee of $7 per student ($13.50 times half a district's student count for administration, three times a year in only reading and mathematics); because the assessments are online, teachers receive the results the next day, so they can immediately use them in their weekly instructional planning. Some districts use three years of NWEA data for high school students to predict scores on college entrance examinations, such as the ACT. Thus, NWEA assessment data might have more utility than just as benchmark or formative assessments, and we would encourage each district to make as much analytic use of such assessment data as possible.

Many Reading First schools use the Dynamic Indicators of Basic Early Literacy Skills (DIBELS) formative assessments (http://dibels .uoregon.edu). Madison, Wisconsin, taught all teachers to use the running records that generally are part of the Reading Recovery tutoring program as the basis for the formative assessment analysis in that district. The Wireless Generation (www.wirelessgeneration.com) has created a formative assessment that can be used with a handheld electronic device. The company offers a web service that provides information on how to turn the results into specific instructional strategies and also provides professional development for teachers, including video clips of how to teach certain reading skills. The cost is about $15 per student per year, plus about $200 per teacher for the device and somewhat more for training, though the company usually uses a trainer-of-trainers approach, where outside groups train individuals who then go out and train others in their district.

Renaissance Learning (www.RenLearn.com) is a leading provider of technology-based school improvement and student assessment programs for K–12 schools. Adopted by more than 70,000 schools, Renaissance Learning's software tools range from daily formative assessment and periodic progress-monitoring technology to norm- and criterion-referenced assessments of reading, early literacy, and math—short cycle assessments that provide interim student achievement data during the school year and are designed for use in instructional planning.

First released in 1996, these short cycle assessments—STAR Reading, STAR Early Literacy, and STAR Math—are now called STAR Enterprise and are the most widely used standardized tests in American schools. Completely computer-administered and computer-adaptive and employing best practices of Item Response Theory, these assessments generate highly reliable and immediate results at any time during the school year for students at widely varying levels of academic achievement, with full comparability of scores from month to month, year to year, and grade level to grade level. Administered entirely on computer and minimizing teacher time, they can be given frequently during the year (e.g., monthly) for screening, monitoring growth and the effectiveness of instruction and intervention, instructional planning, and predicting outcomes on year-end summative assessments. Further, it takes only one Internet-connected classroom computer to operate the system for all students, and the cost is a low $4.25 per student, with modest extra charges for related professional development.

Though the costs of any of these systems vary, $25 per pupil per year is an upward-bound estimate of the ongoing costs (which often include online training and central data analyses) and would be augmented by any additional professional development and onetime expenditures for the hardware to run the systems.

We have not seen districts and schools having trouble with finding the $5 to $25 per pupil for a range of short cycle, formative, diagnostic, and benchmark assessments, most of which are administered in an online, computerized format. Initially, districts can take these dollars from the regular instructional materials budgets, which can average around $175 per pupil per year on a six-year adoption cycle. These interim assessments, including more-detailed diagnostic assessments, also are appropriate expenditures for most categorical programs.

Other School Resources

Schools also need several additional resources—principals, assistant principals in larger schools, secretaries, instructional aides, student support personnel (guidance counselors, social workers, family liaisons, etc.), librarians, and so on. Chapter 2 suggested staffing for these purposes, most of which tend not to be involved in resource reallocation actions. Increasingly in the future, schools will also need access to computer-related information technologies; Chapter 5 addresses the costs and emerging uses and effects of these new approaches.

Summary

This chapter has shown that all schools have multiple opportunities for reassessing current uses of education dollars—mainly the numbers and roles of various staff members in school. But to engage in the process of analyzing the degree to which current resource use aligns with a Plan of Action to improve student performance, *all schools and districts first need clear goals—specific, numeric goals linked to student performance in the core subjects.*

This chapter then argued that many schools and districts have a wide range of options for revising both their Plans of Action and setting priorities for using resources, including the following options:

- taking a flexible approach to class size, as many districts and schools that improved performance and reallocate resources increased class size to mount all their strategies
- rethinking their schedules and number of elective classes while keeping a liberal arts set of curriculum offerings
- carving out time during the regular school day for teacher collaborative work on instructional practice (without late start or early release and without shorting students' instructional time)
- ensuring that all schools have at least some instructional coaches
- placing a high priority on providing individual and very small-group tutoring (one to five students per group) as the prime intervention for struggling students
- rethinking every use of staff in their school

These resource-use priorities should not only boost overall student learning but also close the achievement gaps and reduce the numbers of students identified as having a disability.

Finally, whatever Plan of Action is adopted and however fully that Plan of Action can be staffed, schools and districts need the talent—teachers and principals—to implement the Plan of Action strategy; even more effective talent is needed if their Plans of Action cannot be fully implemented. The next chapter discusses several issues related to the human resource management actions of districts, most of which can be dramatically improved to enhance the effectiveness of all dollars spent on staff, irrespective of their particular roles.

Notes

1. This chapter draws from several sources including Odden (2009), Odden (2011b), Odden and Archibald (2009), and Odden and Picus (2011).

2. This table results from resource needs of Table 3.1 and CPRE Redesign Reports Online, a school reallocation simulation program that models for any school the staffing; see http://cpre.wceruw.org/finance/reports.php.

3. As the book discusses reallocating and cutting staff, readers should know that the process often takes more than one year, that rules and regulations need to be followed, and that staff in areas to be cut or reallocated often have the skills—or can gain the skills through professional development—for the proposed new roles. The point here is that moving staff around involves working with people and therefore must be done with care and respect.

4. Student-teacher ratios are determined by dividing the number of pupils by the *total number of teachers*—core teachers, elective teachers, and many other staff being paid on the teacher salary schedule but not working full-time in classrooms. Thus, student-teacher ratios are much smaller than actual class sizes, which are calculated from the number of students in each class, and exclude the many certified staff in schools who do not actually teach but provide other education functions, such as guidance counselors, instructional coaches, and so on.

4

Recruiting, Developing, and Compensating Top Educator Talent

Local Practices and Supporting State Policies

- Atlanta, Baltimore, Chicago, New York City, Prince Georges County, and several other urban districts across the country have partnered with national teacher and principal talent recruiting organizations to dramatically improve the talent and effectiveness levels of their schools' teachers and principals. These urban districts are now recruiting educators from the top (rather than the bottom) half of the nation's talent pool.

- Scores of districts are experimenting with ways to change both teacher and principal salary structures. Denver, for example, has a totally redesigned salary structure. The Race to the Top program encourages all states to create effectiveness measures for teachers and principals and to use them to change tenure, dismissal, promotion, *and* salary structures.

- Pensions got placed on the state policy agenda in a big way during the 2011 legislative sessions. Though the focus of those sessions was to ask educators to pay a larger portion of pension benefits, the changes are the front end of efforts to rethink educator pensions.

Change is coming to how educators are recruited and hired, evaluated, promoted, tenured, paid, and supported in retirement.

Chapter 4 addresses the issue of educator talent. The fact is that even the best educational improvement strategy will not work if educator talent—largely teachers and principals but also key central office staff—do not have the skills, competencies, and dispositions to implement the strategy. And educator talent is an issue in America. Too many teacher-training programs recruit teacher candidates from the bottom rather than the top half of the undergraduate talent pool; the situation is even worse in the country's large urban schools, many of which have been starved of top teacher and principal talent for decades (Odden, 2011a).

Spending on ineffective teacher and principal talent squanders scarce educational resources. In this era of limited resources, districts and schools need to rethink how they recruit, hire, place, develop, evaluate, retain, dismiss, and pay educator talent. More money should be spent on evaluation systems that identify different levels of teacher and principal effectiveness. Compensation dollars must be used to help create the most effective educational faculty and school leadership as possible. All this requires change in both local practice and state policy, with some initiatives, such as new evaluation systems and performance pay structures, having more immediate effects and others, like pension changes, having longer-term impacts. Better local practices and state policies will ensure that dollars spent on talent will be spent well.

This chapter addresses these issues of educator talent in three sections: one on recruiting, developing, evaluating, and retaining educational talent; a second on revising teacher salary structures to link pay more directly with effectiveness levels; and a third on revising educator pensions to make them fairer and more economically efficient.

Acquiring, Developing, and Retaining Teacher Talent

This section address critical issues related to recruiting, hiring, developing, evaluating, and making decisions on who to retain and who to dismiss. The concepts, recommendations, and policies are discussed in more depth in Odden (2011a), a book focused on the strategic management of human capital in education, addressing the twin goals of improving teaching (instructional practice) and learning (student performance). Each part of this section begins with descriptions of more effective local practice and ends with implications for state policy.

Recruiting

Many school systems in America have a recruitment problem. Unlike the leading countries in the world, such as Korea, Singapore, and Finland, that recruit teachers from the top half—if not solely the top quarter—of the talent pool, the U.S. education system as a whole recruits more teachers from the bottom half of the talent pool.

Urban districts have an even poorer track record. Many urban districts have drawn the bulk of new teachers from local but very low-quality colleges and teacher training programs. Further, until recently, most urban districts did not even review teacher and principal applications until late August, when most solid applicants had already been offered and taken a job elsewhere (Levin & Quinn, 2003). So urban districts hired teachers from the pool of applicants left over in late summer.

Not unexpectedly, many of these individuals proved to be ineffective in the classroom (see, for example, Lankford, Loeb, & Wyckoff, 2002). Nevertheless, the most recent study of teacher evaluation systems concluded that 99+ percent of teachers are found to be satisfactory, accomplished, or advanced, even in districts and schools where student performance is abysmal (Weisberg, Sexton, Mulhern, & Keeling, 2009). To make matters worse, the vast bulk of these individuals are given tenure or some similar job protection such as due process or continuing contract.

Though significant teacher turnover potentially can alleviate some of these problems of staffing schools, the turnover rate for teachers generally is not that all different than in other professions (Harris & Adams, 2007), though turnover rates in urban districts are higher (Lankford et al., 2002). And teacher turnover costs significant resources, estimated from $7,000 to $12,000 per teacher (Milanowski & Odden, 2007; Texas Center for Education Research, 2000). Further, there is some evidence that a larger portion of effective teachers leave early in their careers, rather than a large portion of teachers who are ineffective (Harris & Adams, 2007), leaving the system with decreased level of effectiveness.

Though these staffing problems are much less severe in suburban districts, the general practices are true for the American education system in general. The system recruits from the bottom half rather than the top half of the talent pool; many of those individuals are not effective in teaching students, but nearly everyone receives a positive evaluation, and nearly all of those earn tenure or some equivalent job protection status. All practices represent an ineffective use of the education dollar. These practices must be changed in order for dollars spent on teachers and administrators to be spent effectively.

In the recent past, several urban districts have begun to tackle these educator talent deficiencies. Boston (Archibald, 2008), Chicago (Kimball, 2008), Long Beach (Koppich, 2008), and New York City (Goertz & Levin, 2008) as well as Atlanta, Baltimore, Charlotte-Mecklenburg, and other urban districts have forged new strategies for recruiting better teacher and principal talent. First, they have partnered with national talent recruitment organizations for both teachers, such as Teach For America (Goetz & Aportela, 2008) and The New Teacher Project (Aportela & Goetz, 2008b), and principals, such as New Leaders for New Schools (Aportela & Goetz, 2008a).

Teach For America (TFA) recruits teachers from the country's top universities and places them in high-poverty schools in mostly urban (but also some rural) districts. Indeed, 10 to 15 percent of the graduating classes of Harvard, Princeton, Brown, Duke, Northwestern, and other top-tier colleges and universities across the country apply for a teaching job through TFA, but only one in 10 are accepted. The New Teacher Project (TNTP) recruits early- and mid-career changers from financial services companies, law firms, business consulting firms, and other such organizations and also places them into high-need urban schools.

Research shows these individuals are effective in the classroom, often more effective than teachers entering education through more traditional routes (e.g., Boyd, Lankford, Loeb, Rockoff, & Wyckoff, 2008; Henry et. al., 2010; Noell & Gansl, 2009; Xu, Hannaway, & Taylor, 2008). Other reports find that these teachers exceed the effectiveness of teachers from many universities that have traditionally supplied teachers for urban districts (e.g., Henry et al., 2010; Noell & Gansl, 2009; Tennessee Higher Education Commission, 2010). Similar results have been found for principals prepared by New Leaders for New Schools. Though asking only for a two-year commitment, TFA also finds that 61 percent of those in their program remain in teaching beyond the initial two-year commitment (Teach For America, 2010). These new pathways for educator talent reflect a trend across America—more and more teachers are entering education through alternative pathways; indeed, a recent survey found that since 2005, fully 40 percent of new teacher hires have come through alternative teacher preparation programs (Heitin, 2011).

These districts also have reduced teacher and principal intake from local (but lower-quality) colleges and universities, increased recruitment at higher-quality local universities (the district of Chicago now actively recruits at Northwestern University, University of Chicago, the University of Illinois, and the University of Wisconsin–Madison), sponsored hiring fairs to spur more applications, and launched several other efforts to improve the teacher and principal hiring pool.

Second, these urban districts have moved up the hiring calendar, so schools begin to review applications in February and March, rather than at the end of the summer. In that process, the systems give extra attention to minority applicants and applicants with majors in needed subjects, including mathematics, statistics, and science. The districts have also automated the application process and much of the review process, so applicants feel that they are dealing with a more professional organization.

The result, noted earlier, is that all these districts have increased their teacher and principal talent pool, improved the talent and quality of new hires as well as the overall system, and increased the average level student performance as well as student performance in high-need schools. In short, these revised recruitment strategies have paid off.

However, it is difficult to identify all the costs. Very few districts can identify their costs for recruiting, interviewing, and hiring teachers, and such cost figures in the past would have been not all that meaningful, because the efforts did not target high-quality applicants. Nevertheless, the Milanowski and Odden (2007) study of teacher turnover did identify about $2,600 as the central-office cost of replacing one teacher in a Midwestern urban district. It also found that induction/training costs another approximately $4,500 a teacher, for a total cost of $7,100 to recruit and induct a new teacher.

Recall, that TNTP develops regional recruitment strategies in and around large urban districts, such as Chicago, New York City, and Washington, D.C. TNTP finds that costs depend on the number of new teachers recruited, the subject areas addressed (recruiting math and science is harder, because they are in higher demand), and the level of initial training costs. TNTP estimates that it costs about $6,700 per teacher to recruit a standard cohort of TNTP fellows (75–100 fellows per cohort), but costs can be higher or lower based on the numbers and subjects targeted and the level of training provided. This figure includes the costs of training new recruits over the summer before they start teaching. This cost figure compares quite favorably with the Milanowski and Odden figure of $7,100 per teacher. And there is strong evidence that TNTP recruits top-quality new teachers, while the jury is still out for the recruitment strategies mounted by urban districts themselves.

Teach For America is a more costly operation, but recall that it recruits over the entire nation and recruits only the best and brightest individuals leaving college with new bachelor's degrees. Few school districts in America recruit nationally or just at the best colleges and universities. TFA generally has charged districts about $2,800 for each teacher that the organization recruits, trains, places, and continues to mentor and coach for their first two years of teaching; the per-teacher charge will rise to $5,000 in the near future.

TFA estimates the costs for recruiting, training, and ongoing coaching are approximately $40,000 per teacher, closer to the cost of training a teacher in a university, so the number is harder to compare to just district recruitment costs. However, many of these costs are covered by grants and gifts given to TFA. Moreover, this is the only organization in the country that recruits talent for education solely from the country's top universities, provides training for the each TFA Corps member during the summer before they begin teaching, and also provides ongoing coaching from full-time TFA staff during the first *two* years of their teaching career. Thus, one could argue that the cost could be compared to what good professional development costs (discussed in Chapters 2 and 3), which can reach $14,750 per teacher per year or $29,500 over a two-year period.

So one of the best reasons for a district to partner with TFA to recruit teachers when budgets are tight is that TFA teachers come with a ton of support and investment from the organization itself, none of which the district has to pay for—a fortuitous reality in these times of tight education budgets, when districts are unfortunately cutting professional development budgets and when most districts have never implemented solid new teacher induction programs. At a cost of just $5,000 per new teacher, the district not only is able to hire a very talented teacher but also receives two years of training for those teachers, much of it subsidized by the organizations supporting TFA.

In sum, districts can change how teachers and principals are recruited; they can select higher-quality colleges and universities from which to recruit; partner with national talent organizations such as TFA, TNTP, and New Leaders for New Schools; automate application systems; move up the hiring calendar; and give schools a much better pool of talented individuals with which to fill educator vacancies. Further, the costs of partnering with external organizations for these initiatives are equal to or less than what districts do or should spend on these functions, particularly when initial training and coaching are included. And these organizations are pretty much guaranteed to find top educator talent, which has been a shortcoming for many urban districts in the past.

States can reinforce these district initiatives by legislating the following policies (see Odden, 2011a, for more detail):

- Hike the test score requirements for entry into a teacher training program. Rhode Island and Washington, D.C., have done this; the result has been a reduction in teachers trained in lower-quality colleges and universities and a rise in the quality of newly trained teachers.
- Allow for individuals to enter teaching and administration through nontraditional paths such as Teach For America (TFA), The New Teacher Project (TNTP), and New Leaders for New Schools (NLNS), but make it very rigorous for such individuals to earn a professional license and tenure (discussed below).
- Allow nontraditional organizations such as TFA, TNTP, and NLNS to provide the initial license for teachers and principals but not the professional license.
- Develop incentives for school districts to recruit teachers mainly from the top half of the overall talent pool as a general strategy to improve educator effectiveness.

Teacher Professional Development

Once teachers are hired, they need ongoing professional development. Training is particularly important for new teachers, but professional development is not a one-and-done proposition; it needs to be ongoing as the mix of students change, content and performance standards change, and system expectations continue to rise.

This book has argued that resources for ongoing professional development should be a top priority, even in these tight fiscal times. Instructional practice will not increase systemically unless it is the focus of ongoing systemic attention in a comprehensive professional development program. And such professional development needs to be organized in ways to make it effective—it should lead to change in teachers' instructional practices that produce gains in student achievement. Effective professional development requires pupil-free time for teachers so they can participate in training, time during the regular school day to engage in collaborative work around changing instructional practice, coaching to help teachers to implement new instructional strategies in their classrooms, and resources from either district training or outside consultant training. A new volume by Learning Forward, the national organization focused on professional development, discusses these and many other aspects of what it takes to make professional development work (Crow, 2011).

In that volume, Odden (2011b) specifies that the primary cost elements of effective comprehensive professional development include the following:

- 10 days of pupil-free time for every teacher for training
- $100 per pupil for trainers and administrative costs of mounting professional development
- one instructional coach for every 200 students to provide the onsite assistance teachers and collaborative teams need to transform training into change in classroom practice
- time during the regular school day to work in collaborative teacher groups on instructional issues; this time can be produced when schools also have an appropriate mix of core and specialist/elective teachers. The costs for getting this collaborative time are for the elective teachers and are not included in professional development costs per se (see Odden, 2011b).

Using national average prices, these cost elements total about $14,740 per teacher (approximately $590 per pupil or 5.4 percent of an average district's operating expenditure per pupil).

However, Odden goes on to say that these costs are not all extra costs for many districts. First, most districts already provide some pupil-free days for professional development; teacher salaries would need to be increased slightly to increase the number of pupil-free days to 10. Districts would also need to exert more control over those days, so most (or even all) would be used for ongoing district systemic professional development focused on the curriculum teachers need to teach. Second, many districts have been providing instructional coaches, one of the highest cost elements of effective professional development; districts should keep and expand those coaching positions, because most professional development has little if any impact on teachers' practice, unless it is accompanied with coaching. Many districts have at least some budget for ongoing training. Indeed, several studies have found that many urban districts already spend close to the above figures on teacher professional development (e.g., Miles et al., 2004); such districts need to conduct a professional development program and fiscal audit and then restructure their programs and reallocate current resources to new forms of professional development that work and that are focused on the content and teaching strategies required for the formal curriculum. Such reallocation is much more difficult in rural districts (Thayer, 2004).

Schools and districts also need to think hard about how to organize professional development, including what might be called *new teacher induction programs*. As Chapter 1 argues, the best way to organize teachers—to form the foundation for organizing professional development—is in collaborative work teams inside schools: grade-level teams in elementary schools and subject teams in middle and high schools. These teams analyze student short cycle assessment data (sometimes called *formative assessment data*) to hone and tailor instructional practice, create standards-based curriculum units, and analyze student performance on common end-of-unit tests (to identify both effective and ineffective practices). These teams are the engine for how to improve teaching and instructional practice within schools (Raudenbusch, 2009).

When new teachers are members of such collaborative teams, they gain access to the analytic skills of more experienced teachers, to effective materials that have already been developed and used, to the expertise of fellow teachers, and to individuals who can mentor them on classroom management and expanding their instructional repertoire. If schools have such teams, separate new teacher induction programs are really not needed; new teachers get continuous induction through their participation in their appropriate collaborative team.

To be sure, districts need to organize time for training, both in content and instructional practice. Summer institutes are often the best approach for that training. But having follow-through activities that work largely through teacher collaborative teams is probably the most effective way to ensure that what is included in the up-front training is implemented in all classrooms.

The key policy implication is for states to include in their school finance formulas sufficient funds for new teacher induction/coaching programs or to require 5.4 percent of each district's operating budget to be set aside for the above identified key professional development resources—10 pupil-free days, instructional coaches, and dollars for training.

Evaluation

As noted earlier, most teacher (and principal) evaluation practices do not work—nearly everyone is found to be satisfactory or better, even when student performance is low. However, change seems to be brewing.

Initiatives are being launched across the country to improve the way teachers (and principals) are evaluated. Nearly all efforts plan to use two kinds of measures: indicators of teacher's instructional practice and indicators of teacher impact on student achievement. Milanowski, Heneman, and Kimball (2009) review seven of the systems that measure instructional practice that are currently in use across the country, which states and districts could adapt to their context. Though most state initiatives plan to use some version of a value-added statistic and state accountability tests as the indicators of impact on student learning, there are many other indicators that also could be used as well as other tests such as short cycle interim student assessment scores (Baum, 2011). The goal is to combine multiple indicators in these two arenas—measures of instructional practices and measures of impact on student performance—into overall measures of teacher (and principal) effectiveness, say on a scale of one to five (Milanowski, 2011). The intent is to use these final measures for tenure, promotion, retention, and dismissal and thus turn these important human capital management decisions into strategic decisions, all designed to enhance the effectiveness of educators and the use of the education dollar.

These evaluation initiatives will require some funding. In addition to development and ongoing training costs, the latter of which can be part of comprehensive professional development, one major cost issue is whether the efforts in assessing instructional practice (which include many data items) include *direct observations* of teaching practice or *videos* of such classroom episodes. Though scoring videos is not cost free, using videos is significantly less expensive than requiring live observations. Indeed, the strategies being developed often call for observations of actual classroom practice four to six times a year, sometimes with pre- and postobservation conferences. Such approaches will require scores of observers and cost millions of dollars. Replacing live observations with videos, using a system that is being developed by the Bill and Melinda Gates program on Measuring Effective Teaching and operated by TeachScape (www.teachscape.com), will be much less expensive, even though each video will need to be scored. But the videos also provide a permanent record and can be turned around and used in online development platforms showing various levels of instructional performance and, importantly, instructional practices that are particularly effective.

In addition to state accountability test scores, short cycle interim assessments can also be used to show teacher and principal impact on student learning gains. These assessments are low cost and are needed for the overall education improvement strategy, as Chapter 1 shows. These data can be purchased for under $5 a pupil; the STAR Enterprise system from Renaissance Learning, which is administered online, provides immediate feedback, requires only one computer connected to the Internet, covers reading and math for Grades K–12, and costs just $4.25 a pupil. The assessments can be administered as many times as a teacher desires, compared to the Measures of Academic Progress (MAP) system of Northwest Evaluation Association, which costs almost twice as much.

Once these evaluation systems are developed, teachers and principals would have multiple indicators, each of which can be used to provide formative feedback to help them improve their practice. Each also will have an overall summative score, such as Effectiveness Level 1–5. The intent is to use these summative scores to provide the professional license, tenure, promotion, or dismissal, all based on effectiveness rather than on seniority, and also (as discussed next) to operate new performance pay schedules.

State Policy Implications

States can reinforce these local practices by following these steps:

- Take the lead in developing the core elements of both new teacher evaluations and principal evaluations. Developing these systems requires money, resources, expertise, and time, which most local districts do not have. And the state can create a state team to evaluate all videos of instructional practice. Districts can enhance the core state evaluation with additional local material collected through walk-throughs and data on noninstructional job performance, such as following procedures, implementing policy, and so on (see Milanowski, 2011).
- Develop a multilevel licensure system with at least four levels. Level 1 would be the Initial License. Level 2 would be required for the Professional License; the Professional License would not be provided until the teacher or principal showed that their practice met the standards of Level 2 effectiveness, a much higher bar than requirements for the Initial License.
- Extend the number of years for the tenure decision *and* link tenure to a higher level of practice and effectiveness. If the state had a multitiered licensure system, it could require Level 3 effectiveness as a condition for tenure—a higher bar than the Professional License. This extends the number of

years it takes to earn tenure and allows school systems to acquire much more evidence to make that important decision. And the state could specify that if the educator's effectiveness level ever dropped below Level 3, then he or she would lose tenure and thus possibly his or her job.

- Require that districts dismiss teachers on the basis of effectiveness rather than on seniority, using seniority only if there is a tie between two individuals. One recent study showed that if an effectiveness rather than a seniority criterion were used for layoffs, a different set of teachers would be laid off and fewer layoffs would have been needed as those laid off would have had more years of experience—and a higher salary, and the result would be a faculty with a higher level of overall effectiveness (Goldhaber & Theobald, 2011).

Summary

Many of the dollars in the educational system today are consumed in unconscious ways, particularly those spent on staff. Little attention is given to recruiting teachers and administrators, development systems are too often ineffective, evaluation and tenure practices are soft at best, and promotions and dismissals are often based on seniority rather than effectiveness. This section of the chapter shows how

- recruitment can be strengthened to get better talent into the nation's schools, particularly urban schools
- professional development can be organized and funded to develop changes in classroom practice that will boost student achievement
- evaluation can be restructured to show various levels of effectiveness for both teachers and principals
- new effectiveness metrics can be used to license and tenure only educators who meet high levels of effectiveness. These effectiveness metrics can also be used for promotion and dismissal, which will make dismissal more efficient and increase the overall effectiveness of the remaining educators.

The costs of these initiatives are within the grasp of most school districts, but revised state policies can also help, particularly in developing the evaluation tools to identify the effectiveness levels of key educators, without which better management for acquiring, developing, promoting, and dismissing educational staff cannot be implemented.

Teacher Salary Structures

Teacher salary structures would be strategic if they undergirded the policies and practices outlined in the previous section. To make that happen, the educational system needs to rethink the typical teacher salary schedule. I have argued elsewhere that the current teacher salary schedule is antiquated and does not support current education goals (Odden, 2008a). Beyond the first three or four years, experience is not linked to teacher effectiveness, yet experience or steps in the salary schedule determine how most teacher salary dollars are spent. And except for graduate degrees in the area of licensure, which also consume a hunk of teacher salary resources, neither education units (credits earned at a university before earning a degree) nor degrees are linked to teacher effectiveness. Further, there is nothing linked directly to student performance. As a result, the current teacher salary structure provides weak incentives for the core goals of the educational system—improved teaching and learning.

As the country develops new approaches to teacher evaluation that will include multiple measures of a teacher's instructional practice and multiple indicators of impact on student learning, states and districts will have solid metrics of teacher effectiveness. These metrics can be used not only in evaluation, tenure, retention, and dismissal but also in redesigned teacher salary structures that link pay more to effectiveness levels, thus reinforcing the initiatives on teacher recruitment, development, and retention.

It should be noted that educator pay, or cash compensation, consists of two separate elements—base pay and variable pay. Base pay is the monthly check, usually determined by the salary schedule. The schedule also determines how one earns annual pay increases, which today are usually driven by years of experience and education units/degrees. Variable pay is a bonus, based on improved student performance. Both are important. But too many proposals for changes in how teachers are paid address variable but not base pay, but base pay consumes the most salary dollars.

Table 4.1 shows a new teacher salary schedule operated largely with measures of teacher effectiveness; similar schedules could be developed for principals. There are several points to briefly note about this salary structure, for which the numbers, steps, and columns are only illustrative. First, the various performance categories would be determined by multiple measures of effectiveness—and the higher the effectiveness level, the greater the salary.

Table 4.1   Proposed Teacher Salary Schedule Based on Multiple Measures of Teacher Effectiveness

	Step Within Level	BA	MA	MA30/ Doctorate
Entry	1	$40,000	$41,600	$43,264
Level 1 effectiveness	2	$40,600	$42,224	$43,913
	3	$41,209	$42,857	$44,572
Emerging Professional	1	$45,330	$47,143	$49,029
Level 2 effectiveness	2	$46,010	$47,850	$49,764
	3	$46,700	$48,568	$50,511
	4	$47,400	$49,297	$51,268
	5	$48,112	$50,036	$52,037
	6	$48,833	$50,787	$52,818
Professional	1	$56,158	$58,405	$60,741
Level 3 effectiveness	2	$57,000	$59,281	$61,652
	3	$57,855	$60,170	$62,577
	4	$58,723	$61,073	$63,515
	5	$59,604	$61,989	$64,468
	6	$60,498	$62,919	$65,435
Master	1	$72,598	$75,503	$78,522
Level 4 effectiveness	2	$73,687	$76,635	$79,700
	3	$74,792	$77,785	$80,895
	4	$75,914	$78,951	$82,109
	5	$77,053	$80,136	$83,340
	6	$78,209	$81,338	$84,590

Percent increase for effectiveness level: Level 2: 10%   Level 3: 15%   Level 4: 20%
Percent increase for each step: 1.5%
Math and science incentive: 10%
MA, MA30/Doctorate in license field: 4%
National Board Certification: 10%
MA30 = Master's degree plus an additional 30 units

Second, movement up the schedule is determined by the level of effectiveness. Indeed, this schedule provides the largest pay increases when the effectiveness measures indicate performance at a higher level. This schedule provides accelerating pay increases at each effectiveness level: 10 percent for moving into Level 2, 15 percent for Level 3, and 20 percent for Level 4. Thus, the schedule indicates quite strongly that the major way to earn pay increases is to become more effective. Moreover, the schedule is also designed so that if effectiveness plateaus, so does pay.

Further, if (as discussed earlier) the state specified that teachers would earn the professional license at Level 2 and tenure at Level 3, the salary schedule is quite generous to tenured teachers, but only teachers who remained at effectiveness Level 3 or above would earn such salaries. And the salary for effectiveness Level 4 is even more generous.

Third, young superstars, if they're really effective, could get to the top levels more quickly. As effectiveness indicators showed they met the standards for the next higher performance category, the system could be designed to allow them to skip steps in the schedule and jump up to the higher salary category. For example, assume that every three years each teacher's effectiveness level would be measured. A hotshot could enter the system at Level 1, Step 1, and move to Level 2, Step 2 after three years. But after just another 3 years, if their effectiveness rose to Level 3, they could jump up to Level 3, Step 1. Their salary at the new level would not only include the three 1.5 percent step increases that they jumped, but also include the 15 percent increase for moving into Level 3 effectiveness. And three years later, if their effectiveness level rose to the top—Level 4—they could then jump to the entry salary of Level 4, garnering the cumulative three 1.5 percent step increases plus the 20 percent for entering the top effectiveness level.

On the other hand, salaries are capped (except for periodic market adjustments) by the top step in each effectiveness level, so if a teacher's effectiveness stays at Level 3, his or her salary will always be lower than the salary for teachers in Level 4.

A significant policy decision for districts would be to determine what to do if a teacher's effectiveness indicator fell below that for Level 3; should the salary then be dropped to an appropriate step in Level 2? There would be a similar issue for dropping from Level 4 to Level 3. If, however, a state required Level 3 performance to earn—as well as retain—tenure, then the salary issue for dropping to Level 2 would be resolved, as the teacher would not retain his or her tenure and thus his or her job if effectiveness dropped below Level 3. The district would still need to determine how to handle the salary for a drop in performance from Level 4 to Level 3.

Fourth, this schedule shows some step increases within each level; fewer or more steps could be provided, but the highest step in each category is—and should be—lower than the first step in the next-highest effectiveness level.

Fifth, this basic structure can be augmented with incentives for teachers in areas for which there are teacher shortages, such as math and science, as well as provide an additional incentive for certification from the National Board for Professional Teaching Standards. In other research, we have suggested salary incentives of at least an additional $5,000 for teachers in areas for which there are shortages, such as mathematics and science, as well as for schools in high-need areas (Milanowski, 2008a; Odden, 2008a).

This structure would transform how teachers are paid by linking the level of pay to the level of effectiveness, a goal long sought by policymakers and education leaders. In addition, a salary structure of this type is affordable by almost all school districts if they reallocate current salary dollars to this structure over time (Odden, 2008a), assuming the overall system develops the multiple effectiveness indicators needed to operate it. A similar structure could be developed for principals.

Moreover, school systems could use such structures and *not* provide automatic pay increases every year. Automatic pay increases were fine in the past, when the nation's economy—and state and local taxes—grew every year; but that no longer happens. Therefore, automatic pay raises should be curtailed. Each year, a district could first determine how much additional money was available for salaries. The district would then decide priorities for salary increases, such as funding all effectiveness level increases first, then subject-area shortages, then step increases, and then any appropriate market adjustment. But these decisions would best be made every year in order to ensure that greater salary expenditures could be afforded (i.e., that districts had a budget to fund them). Once automatic pay increases are allowed (the situation today in most districts), every year requires a larger budget before key decisions can are made about programs, salaries, and what can be afforded.

In addition, bonus programs for individual teachers or all faculty in grades or schools could—and we argue should—be provided on top of these base salary schedules (Milanowski, 2008b). Such bonus programs would require a separate budget over and above that for the salary schedule.

Both the revised salary schedule and a bonus program based on student achievement are needed, the former to pay for the assets teachers bring to the system—instructional expertise—and the latter as a direct payment for increasing student performance beyond historical trends. In this way, the cash components of educator compensation would be directly linked to the twin goals of most educational systems—improving teaching (i.e., instructional practice) and student achievement. Together, these approaches to compensation would structure base pay for teachers and principals on their instructional (or leadership) effectiveness and provide bonuses for directly improving student performance; they would also spend salary dollars much more strategically than they are spent today.

Summary and State Policy Implications

The time has come to change teacher (and principal) salary systems so that the prime pay increases are linked to the key goals of the educational system—improved teaching and increased student performance. New approaches to educator evaluation, which include multiple measures of both instructional practice and impact on student learning gains, provide the metrics to operate such new salary schedules. The new schedules could then be augmented with incentives for teachers in subject-area shortages as well as for working in high-poverty, hard-to-staff schools. The result would be to form a stronger link between educator salary levels and educator effectiveness.

To support these teacher salary changes, states could do the following:

- provide incentives for districts to restructure salary schedules to operate on effectiveness measures rather than on years of experience
- develop statewide minimum salary schedules with minimum salary amounts for each effectiveness levels, thereby specifying the general structure of redesigned teacher salary structures
- launch similar initiatives for administrator salary structures

Educator Pensions

In the short term, pension costs cannot be impacted much by local educators, as pensions are structured and regulated primarily by state governments. Nevertheless, pension costs are significant and growing. Pension costs should neither be considered a given nor something inappropriate for local educator thought. Especially in these times of constrained budgets, pension costs should be scrutinized and pension benefits analyzed as every education expenditure is closely reviewed with an eye toward making the spending more effective.

Indeed, pensions are an important part of educator compensation, just like they are in other public and private sector compensation schemes. Unlike the private sector, where pensions have been reduced, switched from defined benefit programs to defined contribution programs, or even eliminated, educators—both teachers and administrators—continue to have significant retirement benefits. Nearly all retired teachers and administrators have some version of a (usually generous) pension, typically a defined benefit pension, and many retired educators also have health benefits above and beyond the federal Medicare program (Hansen, 2010).

These benefits require substantial funding; indeed, both pension and retiree health benefits have been consuming larger and larger portions of school operating budgets (Costrell & Podgursky, 2009): pensions because their structure boosts costs by allowing teachers to retire far before the normal retirement age of sixty-six, and health benefits because they were not budgeted years ago when they were offered, but with today's accounting rules, require a budget (Clark, 2010).

To address these pension issues, this section is divided into three parts: (1) an overall description of three major kinds of pensions; (2) an analysis of the incentives built into typical teacher pension programs and the impacts of these structural features on pension payouts, teacher mobility, and educator effectiveness; and (3) a recommendation for making educator pensions both fairer to everyone and more predictably affordable.

Three Major Pension Structures and the Typical Educator Pension

There are three major types of pensions in both public and private sectors. The first is Defined Benefit (DB) programs, which provide retirees with a specific pension benefit. As shown in Table 4.2, the benefit amount is typically calculated on the basis of the number of years of service, an average final salary (often the average of the highest three- to five-year salaries in education), and a multiplier for each year of service, such as 2.0 percent. So a person with 30 years of experience, an average salary for the highest three to five years of $70,000, and a multiplier of 2.0 percent would have a beginning pension of $42,000 ($70,000 times 2 percent times 30 years, or 60 percent of the

Table 4.2   Retirement Calculation for a Defined Benefit Pension

Total Years of Experience	Multiplier	Average Final Salary	Beginning Pension Annual Salary
30	2.0	$70,000	$42,000
30 times	2.0 = 60% times	$70,000	= $42,000

final average salary). The initial pension is then adjusted annually, sometimes by a fixed percentage (which, over time, is expensive) and sometimes linked to the performance of the system's pension fund. Only in rare cases can the DB be transferred from one state to another. Thus, educators who do not stay in one state for their entire career experience pension penalties, because any pension earned at the time of leaving for another job is not increased over time, and so is eroded by inflation.

By contrast, a Defined Contribution (DC) program, such as a 401(k) program in the private sector or a 403(b) program in the public sector, offers a specified pension contribution each year (for example, 5 percent from the employee and 10 percent from the employer), with those amounts placed into a personal pension account, usually monthly. The pension, then, is the lump sum of this account, which equals all of the contributions over the period of work and the accumulated investment gains; the lump sum can be used to purchase an annuity (an annual pension payment) or can be managed to provide a certain payout monthly. Further, most DC plans allow the worker to retain the pension if they move to another district or state, so there is no penalty for moving across pension systems, as is the case with DB plans.

The difference between the two is that the DB plan offers a specified annual pension amount at retirement, irrespective of who contributed what amount to the pension fund over time and irrespective of the performance of the pension fund, while the DC plan offers a specified annual contribution, with the amount of the pension depending on contributions and the investment performance of the pension account over the work life of the individual. In theory, both could provide the same ultimate pension amount, but in practice, they rarely do.

Further, the DB plan puts the burden for providing the pension on the organization (the government, in the case of educator pensions), and the DC plan puts the burden for the pension on the individual and how he or she manages his or her pension account. Moreover, DB plans morph into the underfunded arena when governments fail to provide their annual contribution, which over time can cause significant pension funding shortfalls, or when the political system provides pension enhancements at some point in time without proper funding for them. DC plans are susceptible to poor management, as not every individual is a wise investor, and critical mistakes can cause an investment fund to lose huge amounts of money. Finally, as noted earlier, DC plans cater to educators who are mobile across states or districts, while DB plans are not.

By contrast, Cash Balance (CB) pension programs, which are growing in many private sector organizations, offer a nice compromise between the above two options, and as is argued below, can make educator pensions much fairer, eliminate the early retirement and high-cost incentives that exist today in too many educator pensions, and forge a strong and appropriate link between pension payouts and contributions and related investment gains.

CB programs work in part like a DC plan: the employee and employer each makes a pension contribution annually. That amount is placed into an individual's personal pension account, and the pension dollars are invested. But the pension dollars are managed by a neutral external entity, and the plans usually guarantee an annual return, which traditionally has been about 6 percent, a conservative figure by historical measures (though a generous figure in these times of economic stress and volatile stock and bond markets). Further, most CB are portable like DC plans, and so cater to individuals who do not work in the same job for their entire career, a characteristic of today's workers (O'Toole & Lawler, 2006), including teachers (Pew Research Center, 2010). At retirement, the individual can decide how to split the total value of the pension account between an annuity that pays an annual pension amount and investments earnings that accrue each year. So CB plans are very much like DC plans but place the burden for pension management onto an external expert body—which could be a body such as the Wisconsin Employee Trust Fund, which manages very well and very expertly the investment portfolios that pay pensions for Wisconsin retirees. CB plans also guarantee a minimum return. See Table 4.3 for a summary of the key features of DB, DC, and CB pension plans.

Impacts of Typical Educator Pensions on Teacher Behavior and Pension Costs

As stated previously, all three of the above plans could work the same way; in practice, that is not the case. Educator pensions have several elements that raise pension costs, separate benefits from contributions and accrued investment gains, redistribute pension dollars from younger to older teachers, and might negatively impact educator

Table 4.3 Key Features of DB, DC, and CB Pensions

Pension Feature	Defined Benefit (DB)	Defined Contribution (DC)	Cash Balance (CB)
Employer contribution	Yes	Yes	Yes
Employee contribution	Yes	Yes	Yes
Responsibility for pension fund management	Government	Individual	Government
Guaranteed minimum investment return	No	No	Generally yes
Portable across state lines	Generally no	Generally yes	Yes
Pension payment aligned with pension contributions and investment gains	Often no	Yes	Yes
Fixed pension payment	Yes	No	No
Pension payment depends on total contributions and investment gains	No	Yes	Yes
Pension payment adjusted appropriately for early or late retirement	Generally no	Yes	Yes

quality. For all these reasons, this section concludes by recommending changes in educator pensions.

How pensions should work. Pensions are designed to provide a retired educator with a retirement income of some level. The idea is to have the educator and the school system, whether the district or the state, contribute an amount to a pension fund each year, with those contributions and the accrued investment gains funding the pension benefit at retirement. If a person started work at age 25 and worked 40 years to age 65, the value of the amount contributed and accrued from investment practices for that individual would then fund the pension; the amount would be determined by an actuarially calculated figure that estimated the number of years the retired educator would live and receive the pension.

If the person retired somewhat early, such as at age 62, which is allowed by Social Security, the accrued pension amount at retirement would be less (as the person would have worked three fewer years), and the person would be on average expected to receive a pension for an additional three years; for both these reasons, early retirement usually carries with it a significant reduction in the amount of the pension, so that the total present value of the pension received would be equal for the person retiring early or at 65. A similar calculation would be made for retiring after age 65.

The concept would be to make calculations of the net present value of the pension payout the same and fully aligned with pension contributions and accrued investment gains over the work life of the individual educator. In this way, there would be a smooth curve of pension benefits earned over the work life of the individual. And if the individual retired very early, say at age 50 or 55, the early retirement reduction would be substantial—the pension benefit would be what could be purchased with the much smaller pension accrual at that very early age.

There are several pension elements that cause most educator pensions not to behave in the above rational way (Costrell & Podgursky, 2009, 2010), each discussed below.

Artificially increasing final average salary. Because the typical educator pension is based on some final average salary figure (often the average of the highest three or so years but sometimes simply the highest year), that average can be and has been significantly artificially increased. For example, an individual could be made a department chair for their last year and be given a large pay increase; that would inflate the final average salary above historic trends. Some districts pay educators an amount linked to accumulated but unused sick leave; these payments, which can be quite large, are included in the last year's salary and artificially inflate the average salary calculation. Other districts promote administrators for just the final year or add to the salary an amount that previously was provided for additional pensions. All these practices create spikes in the final salary, artificially inflate the final average salary figure, boost pension costs, and break the link between pension accruals and pension payouts.

These last-year salary spikes have much, much smaller impacts on the portfolio value for either DC or CB programs.

Early retirement specifications. The typical educator pension also allows teachers and administrators to retire with full (or only modestly reduced) benefits significantly before the normal Social Security retirement age of 67 (which most policy analysts now say should be raised to as high as 70 to ensure the fiscal stability of that federal pension program). Often these early retirement rules kick in at about age 50, using what states call the rule of 75 or 80. The rule states that if the sum of the educator's age (say, 50) and years of experience (say, 30) is equal to or greater than 75 or 80, then the educator can retire at full benefits (to be sure, at his or her actual average final salary level at that point) but without early retirement reductions. Though a lower salary at age 50 would produce a pension benefit lower than the average final salary at age 65, the educator would receive the pension for an additional 15 years, which in almost all cases more than balances a somewhat higher pension at age 65. Further, some states even inflate years of experience for such early retirees or even the multiplier, further enhancing the net benefit of early retirement. As a result, the long-term value of the pension benefit spikes up for many educators in many states in their early 50s, providing strong incentives for teachers to retire at that time in their work life.

Though more research is needed, economists argue that these strong incentives not to retire until one reaches an age in the early 50s nor to postpone retirement until 65, can potentially incent ineffective teachers to hang on to an education job until eligible for early retirement as well as incent effective teachers to retire early. Whatever labor market behaviors result from these early retirement incentives, they are at strong odds with a pension system that would be neutral with respect to a specific retirement age or designed to maximize the effectiveness of educators in the educational system (Costrell & Podgursky, 2009; Friedberg & Turner, 2010).

Further, though the pension benefits that accrue prior to becoming eligible for early retirement are aligned with pension contributions and accumulated investment gains, the huge spikes in pension benefits during the early retirement period are above that normal accrued value—and must be funded from some source. However funded, such stipulations provide retirement benefits that far exceed pension contributions and investment gains, thus adding significantly to pension fund costs and inequities in the distribution of pension benefits.

Vesting requirements. One source of funding these higher pension costs derives from vesting requirements combined with educator mobility. Many states require educators (and school systems) to pay into pension funds as soon as they start teaching but require educators to work in the system for a number of years—say, 5 to 10—before they actually qualify for a pension (i.e., before pension benefits vest). But many educators, especially younger teachers, leave teaching before the pension vests with them. However, the educational system's contributions for these leaving teachers remain in the pension fund, thus financing pensions for others who remain a longer time and at some point actually draw a pension.

Further, even if a younger teacher remains in the system until the pension vests and then leaves the system, the pension benefit is linked to their final average salary at that point—and does not rise with inflation over time. Moreover, in order to obtain this pension (often two to three decades later), the educator would need to leave their individual pension contribution in the system. But neither that nor the system's contribution would earn interest or be adjusted by pension fund investment gains over the next few decades, so the pension payout is far below pension contributions and investment gains. Thus, most rational educators decide not to take these small pension amounts. Though they are allowed to take their individual contributions with them as they move to another job, they can take only their own contributions—not the educational system's contributions—and they usually receive their own contributions with no investment gains. So young mobile teachers experience significant long-term pension penalties.

The result is that educators who do not stay in one educational system (or state) for their entire career but move from one system to another are severely disadvantaged when it comes to drawing a real pension at a normal retirement age. Indeed, there was a chief state school officer who served in several states as well as the U.S. Department of Education and was eligible for just a pittance of a pension when he faced retirement age, all a result of these inequitable, structural pension issues.

Costrell and Podgursky (2010) have estimated that about half an entering teacher's pension wealth is redistributed to teachers who retire in their fifties as compared to educators who leave the educational system before that (and work in another state but still in education). They further estimate that teachers who simply work in two districts in two different states with two different pension systems have half the net pension wealth of teachers who work the same number of years in one pension system. The penalty of even this modest level of mobility, which is certainly not unusual, is huge and unfair.

Summary. In sum, the way most educator DB educator pensions work increases pension costs, encourages possible ineffective teachers to stay in teaching until their early fifties, encourages effective teachers to retire in their fifties rather than stay in teaching, discriminates against educators who do not stay in the same pension system (district/state) for their entire career, redistributes dollars from young to older teachers, inhibits teacher mobility across state lines, and breaks the link between pension contributions and accrued investment gains and pension payouts. As a result, typical educator pension systems push against rather than support efforts to continually enhance the effectiveness of the educator workforce.

In short, educator pensions need to be structurally changed to make them fairer, more economically efficient, more aligned with worker mobility across states and jobs in the 21st century, and more supportive of efforts to increase educator talent level and effectiveness.

A Proposal for Improving Educator Pensions

The private sector not only within the United States but also around the world has shifted pensions from Defined Benefit to Defined Contribution pension programs. DC pension programs, moreover, have some attractive properties. First, they can vest with the individual immediately and include both the individual and the organization's contribution. Second, DC plans are portable, meaning they are owned by the individual and can serve as a depository for any pension benefits earned in another organization or system. Thus, DC plans are more aligned with a workforce that is mobile, which also is the case for educators today.

Further, when funded monthly, DC pension programs eliminate any unknown or difficult-to-predict future liabilities for an actual pension payout that is associated with DB programs. This is one of the reasons the private sector has shifted to DC plans; they then have no future pension liability. However, this shift puts the burden for pension payouts on individuals as they must manage their pension fund and then also manage their pension account structure when it begins to payout. And as stated earlier, not everyone has the skills and wisdom to manage a pension account wisely. In fact, most would argue that this shift of responsibility could be disastrous if large percentages of individuals make unwise investment decisions.

For these reasons, this book and increasing numbers of economists (e.g., Costrell & Podgursky, 2010) recommend that states shift educator pensions to Cash Balance (CB) pension programs. CB programs have all the attractive features of DC programs but shift pension fund management to an expert entity. This ensures that the pension dollars will be invested wisely and should grow over the work life of an individual and be able to purchase an annuity that will serve as a generous fully funded pension when the educator retires.

CB programs, as well as DC programs, also have two more attractive features. They are fully aligned with pension contributions and accumulated investment gains over the work life of an individual and so are economically fair. And they are aligned with lower or higher pension payouts if an individual decides to retire early or late. Early retirees will be able to purchase an annuity with the lower amount that would be in their pension fund at the time of early retirement (and would not experience the pension benefit spikes that are now available in so many pension programs for educators in their early fifties). The pension fund total value for late retirees would be higher and could be used to purchase a higher annual pension benefit; indeed, since both the pension fund would be larger and the average number of years to death would be lower, a later retiree would be able to purchase a significantly higher annuity.

CB programs would also help undergird the development of a more-national recruitment system for teachers and administrators. As organizations like Teach For America, The New Teacher Project, and New Leaders for New Schools recruit nationally for teacher and principal talent and place such individuals nationally, a CB pension program would allow such individuals to acquire pension wealth all through their work life, whether they move from one educational system to another or leave education after some time. There would be no pension penalty for not working in one place for 30 to 40 years, such as is the case today for most DB pension programs.

Monahan (2010) argues that these proposed pensions changes would be legal in this country, at least for new educators and pension benefits going forward for educators now in educational systems. She argues that current law and case findings imply that pension benefits that have accrued are hard—and perhaps impossible—to change retrospectively, unless governments or pension programs go through a bankruptcy proceeding, like many airlines and automobile and other companies did; then pension obligations can be modified.

Shifting to CB programs will not resolve current unfunded pension liabilities; they will have to be addressed on their own. But shifting to CB pension programs would improve educator pension systems in many ways and at least avoid unfunded liabilities in the future.

Summary

States shifting educator pensions to Cash Balance pension programs could improve educator pensions in the future. Cash Balance educator pensions would

- be fair to all educators
- align pension benefits with pension contributions and investment gains
- entail no pension wealth redistribution from younger to older educators
- fit with the mobile workforce of the global economy today
- undergird multiple state as well as national efforts to raise the talent and effectiveness levels of teachers
- ensure a fairer distribution of teacher and principal talent not only within school districts and states but also across the country

Moreover, CB pension programs are neutral with respect to the age at which an individual retires and so allows individuals to retire whenever they want, with the retirement annuity equal to what their total account balance could purchase, though early retirement would provide a lower annuity but commensurate with pension contributions and investment gains over the working life of the individual. Finally, CB pension programs appeal more to the millennials now entering the workforce, including the educational system (DeArmond & Goldhaber, 2010).

Though such a pension shift would not save education dollars in the short term, it should help mitigate the continually increasing costs of pension programs caused by the elements of typical DB pension programs discussed earlier and make pensions a stable element of school budgets. Further, such a shift could have the pension system reinforce rather than inhibit the many human capital initiatives school systems are launching to raise the talent and effectiveness levels of teachers and administrators (Odden, 2011a), including the recruitment, evaluation, and performance-based pay programs discussed in the first and second sections of this chapter.

5

Computers and Technology in Education

Costs and Online Options

- Florida, Idaho, and several other states now require all students to take one online course in order to graduate from high school.
- All Advanced Placement (AP) courses are now available online, so any student in any high school in any state has access to all AP classes, if there is an Internet-connected computer in the school.
- *Blended-learning classrooms*, which combine face-to-face and online learning in large classrooms, are popping up all over the country, including such places as Rocketship Mateo Sheedy Elementary School in San Jose, California, a high-poverty, high–English language learner (ELL) school that now ranks as one of the highest-performing elementary schools in the state.
- Appleton, Wisconsin, has created several virtual charter schools, each of which costs around just $6,000 to $7,000 per pupil for the entire K–12 curriculum, as compared to the nearly $11,000 per pupil that districts in Wisconsin spend on average.

- The international publishing giant Pearson has partnered with the Bill and Melinda Gates Foundation to provide an online curriculum for the new common reading and mathematics standards.
- The Khan Academy offers to anyone, free of charge, over 2,700 videos on many subjects including elementary mathematics, algebra, calculus, and accounting. In May 2011, the website had more than 2 million visitors, dwarfing any traditional online education site.

The U.S. educational system is being buffeted by more sophisticated, cheaper-than-the-typical-public-school, online-delivered instructional programs than ever in its history. Most of the systems are stunningly effective in producing student achievement for some—though not all—students, but more and more programs are working even in high-poverty, traditionally low-performing environments. In short, highly effective and lower-cost technology-driven instruction programs are creeping onto the education landscape all across the country. This should be viewed as a fortuitous phenomenon in these challenging times when the pressure to improve student performance continues even as most education budgets are being cut.

Chapter 5 provides an overview of the various online learning options that are rapidly expanding across the K–12 education system. The first section of this chapter identifies the costs of equipping schools with the technology infrastructure needed to fully support the delivery and implementation of these new curricula. The second section gives a broad outline of existing online programs while focusing on the key attributes and cost-effectiveness of three leading models: state-supported virtual schools, private sector technology-based solutions, and blended classes.

This chapter shows that current widely available technologies can be repurposed to educate many (though not all) students in ways that are considered as effective as and less costly than the traditional classroom. Given the current political and fiscal climate, it would be prudent for states, districts, and schools to strongly consider incorporating one or more of these models into their existing curriculum and instructional strategies. Cost-effective instructional delivery is not simply a possible goal today for many districts—it is a necessity.

Costs of Technology Software and Hardware[1]

Over the last five years, technology has become a more integral part of K–12 education (Pew Research Center, 2010). Students use more devices than ever before; they multitask and communicate through new media mechanisms. Data-capable phones and other small, form factor computers that can all connect to the Internet allow students more access to resources and information.

Research has identified four major benefits of technology: (1) more student preparation to enter the workforce or higher education, (2) higher levels of student motivation, (3) increased student learning or academic achievement, and (4) increased teacher/student access to resources (Earle, 2002; Roblyer, 2005). Technology can motivate students to become self-directed learners, increasing time on task, quality of work, and attendance. New software techniques that promote student interaction and use elements of computer gaming, coupled with teacher assignments that leverage the strengths of technology, promote active learning and encourage students to become more independent learners (Prensky, 2010). Technology proficiency is becoming a necessity for students to compete locally and globally in higher education, business, and the general workforce (Schrum & Levine, 2009; U.S. Department of Education, 2010b).

Cost Overview

Infusing technology into the school curriculum means taking into account the associated costs for the computer hardware, networking equipment, software, training, and personnel associated with maintaining and repairing these machines. The *total cost* of purchasing and embedding technology into the operation of schools identifies both the direct and indirect costs of technology and its successful implementation. The *direct costs* of technology include hardware, software, and labor costs for repairing and maintaining the machines, which is the focus of this section. *Indirect costs* include the costs of user support, time spent in training classes, casual learning, self-support, user application development, and downtime costs. This section discusses only direct technology costs, as the indirect costs (primarily training) are included in the overall discussions about professional development discussed in Chapter 2. Districts also need individuals to serve as technical support for technology-embedded curriculum and management systems, though the bulk of that work can be covered by warranties purchased at the time the computers are acquired.

The main goal of the following analysis is to identify the direct costs of purchasing, upgrading, and maintaining the computer technology hardware, the software that allows these computers to function, and the networks on which they run. This analysis recognizes the reality that today virtually no school is beginning at a baseline of zero. All schools have a variety of computers of varying ages, the large majority of which are connected to school networks and the Internet (U.S. Department of Education, 2010a). Unlike the 1990s, when expensive projects had to retrofit schools with data networks, the following cost analysis identifies resources needed to maintain and enhance the technology base that exists in schools. Moreover, as should be clear, these are ongoing and not onetime costs.

It also is noted that each district and school situation is unique, requiring that an individual technology plan be created at both district and school levels. Most districts and schools already have technology plans because of the federal funding requirements in the E-Rate and Enhancing Education Through Technology (EETT) programs. These plans should be used as meaningful mechanisms to allocate resources to the areas of most need within the school or district environment.

The following estimates four categories of technology costs that total $250 a pupil. The amounts by category should be considered flexible, as districts and schools will need to allocate dollars to their highest-priority technology needs outlined in state and district technology plans. The following are per-pupil costs for each of the four subcategories:

- computer hardware: $71
- operating systems, productivity, and noninstructional software: $72
- network equipment, printers, and copiers: $55
- instructional software and additional classroom hardware: $52

Computer Hardware

The estimated annual cost per pupil for *computer hardware* is $71, calculated using an average cost of $850 per computer, a 3-to-1 student-to-computer ratio, and a four-year average replacement cycle. To arrive at the $71 per-pupil figure, the average cost of the computer ($850) was divided by the average computer life span (four years), producing a figure of $213, which was divided by the student-to-computer ratio (3), yielding the result of $71.

At first glance, the $850 figure might seem high, but it is derived from the average price of a computer within a group of machines that could include desktop workstations, laptops, servers, high-end video editing stations, and/or wireless mobile carts (20 laptops and cart at $25,000), depending on school site needs. This figure assumes a three-year onsite warranty for each computer, which reduces personnel costs for tech support and leaves highly technical problems to expert private companies. It also provides at least a 17-inch LCD monitor for each computer to reduce eyestrain. Each computer should be purchased with the most up-to-date operating system and the latest office productivity suite ($50) preinstalled, so computers will only need to be reconfigured, not reimaged, at installation.

Although a four-year replacement cycle for most applications in educational technology is adequate, many computers can be used beyond this time frame. For example, for computers used for simple word processing and other such tasks, a five-year replacement cycle (especially with the software replacement outlined below) is appropriate. On the other hand, some secondary classrooms—higher mathematics, art, biology, and some career-tech programs like Project Lead The Way—require the latest available technology and should be refreshed on a three-year cycle. Further, because the student-to-computer ratios include computers for administrators and office staff, "power users" in the school office, such as the individual who processes student data, may require a three-year replacement.

With the 3-to-1 ratio used in this analysis, a school has enough computers to create one or more computer laboratories (depending on the size of the school) and provide four to five workstations in each classroom for reference or small-group projects as well as for taking short cycle interim assessments. The 3-to-1 student-to-computer ratio can be lowered by stretching the life span of each computer past a four-year cycle, using older machines for simpler tasks such as word processing or basic Internet access, and using faster machines in classrooms where software demands are higher.

Further, in the near future it will be possible to use devices like iPads for foreign language classes and class projects across the curriculum, in which short videos and other sound clips could be used to produce multimedia productions. Currently, Apple is offering a class set of 25 iPads to schools for about $8,500, an average of about $340 a machine. However, it should be noted that iPads still lack the ability to use common productivity software such as word processors and that the ability for a teacher to actively manage these computers is limited to nonexistent. Therefore, although these devices may serve specific instructional uses, they are still not a replacement for a desktop or laptop computer, and they are substantially more expensive than standard net books, which actually may provide more functionality for students.

Finally, some educators urge lowering the 3-to-1 student-to-computer ratio to 2-to-1 or even 1-to-1, which would dramatically increase costs. One-to-one programs require more computers, personnel, networking, electrical, and other associated costs. Start up and maintenance costs of laptop programs are major barriers to moving to 1-to-1. Start-up costs are high, because the existing computer base of desktop units cannot be used to offset the initial expenditures of laptops for all students; thus, each student requires a new laptop when a 1-to-1 computer-to-student program starts. Assuming the cost of a new laptop (extended replacement warranty, initial software, etc.) is $1,000 and assuming a four-year replacement cycle, the cost of the computer alone is $250 per pupil per year.

One of the postulated benefits of laptop programs is an assumed cost savings in textbooks. The rationale is that electronic textbooks are cheaper than printed editions. Though a compelling argument, it is hard today to fully realize such savings. First, not all textbook companies provide electronic versions of their texts; if not all texts are available in electronic format, savings are reduced. Second, most textbook companies provide only minimal discounts for the electronic version versus the printed version of the book, so there is little savings in purchasing the electronic version.

Operating System, Productivity, and Noninstructional Software

This category consists of diverse software packages that allow computers to run, protect networks, and provide students with productivity tools to help them formulate and communicate their ideas. When productivity and system software packages were initially developed (Windows, Microsoft Word, etc.) major revisions to these products were released every few years. However, as the software has matured over the last 20 years, programs have been fine-tuned, and major revisions are less frequent. Many times, software will outlast the useful life of a computer. And, with the Internet used as a delivery mechanism, minor revisions for many of these products can be installed at no charge as soon as the companies make them available.

The following identifies $57 per pupil as the annual cost of upgrading operating systems and productivity suites (e.g., Microsoft Office) as well as server software. To determine this figure, software was divided into three groups, depending on whether the products are priced on a subscription, a per-workstation, or a per-pupil charge.

Group A. Group A consists of software packages that are billed on a onetime subscription basis. Since the cost is a onetime charge, the amount should be divided by the number of years that the product is useful. Today, most of these software products have at least a five-year useful life cycle before a major revision is released. Considering a four-year computer replacement cycle, this means that many computers might use the same operating system or productivity software, without ever requiring a major software revision. Other computers, however, are in the middle of their useful life when a new major software revision comes forth. To update the software on these computers, a district or school would need to pay for the new revision. Therefore, it is probable that at least 50 percent of the computers will need to receive a software upgrade during their useful life.

To determine the costs for this category, the annual calculation for the software in Group A is based on the approximate cost of the software package divided by 2 (because half of the computers would receive a purchased major upgrade during their useful life span). This halved cost was then placed in Table 5.1, next to the software type listed in Group A. Next, the halved prices were added together to produce a subtotal for Group A. This subtotal was then divided by five to give an average annual cost of the major revision per workstation spread over the five-year useful life of the revision. Finally, the annualized cost was divided by three to accurately represent the cost of one workstation shared by three pupils (3-to-1 student-to-computer ratio).

Server operating software, part of Group A, is much more expensive, but the same factors apply to these products that apply to the rest of Group A. These servers, such as file and database servers, require client access licenses in addition to the regular licenses. Larger campuses have at least two servers with various services running. After averaging in the number of servers provided at the district level, the formula for this category assumes three servers per school site.

Group B. Group B includes software that can be purchased on a per-workstation charge. Antivirus software, Internet content filters, backup executive software, remote access software, recovery software, and laboratory management software are all elements of

Table 5.1   Costs of Operating, Productivity, and Noninstructional Software

Group A	
Five-year refresh cycle	
Operating systems	$20
Productivity suits	$30
Servers	$800
Subtotal Group A	$850
Group A divided by five-year refresh cycle	$170
Group A five-year cycle figure divided by (3-to-1 student-to-computer ratio)	$57
Group A per-pupil annual expenditure	$57
Group B	
Annual subscription basis (per workstation)	
Antivirus	$8
Other network costs (content filter, etc.)	$5
Subtotal Group B	$13
Group B subtotal divide by 3 (3-to-1 student-to-computer ratio)	$4
Group B per-pupil annual expenditure	$4
Group C	
Annual subscription basis (per pupil)	
Calling system	$3
Student administration	$5
Financial system	$3
Subtotal Group C	$11
Group C per-pupil annual expenditure	$11
Annual per-pupil total of Groups A, B, and C	$72

Group B. This group of software is not directly seen by users but is vital for technicians. Without these tools, personnel costs to maintain the computers and networks would rise dramatically. Internet security software, which protects district students, computers, and servers from e-mail viruses, electronic threats, spam, and undesirable Internet content, is vital. Many of these services can be purchased separately or in suites.

The annual per-pupil expenditure calculation for Group B requires that the group subtotal be divided by three (to spread the expenditures to the three students per workstation represented in a 3-to-1 student-to-computer ratio), resulting in a figure of $4 per student.

Group C. Group C software products are usually based on an annual per-pupil model. although there are exceptions. One example within the group is the student administration system, which is vital to the school system. The need for student administration systems is clear. The cost per year varies depending on the modules that a school wants to purchase. Possible modules include grading programs, teacher websites for posting homework, online registration for classes for secondary schools, and/or web-based attendance programs that allow parents to have instant access to their child's attendance history.

Mass dialing systems have become more commonplace over the last five years. Earlier systems were school or district based, requiring on-site technical support and additional phone lines to allow for high-volume calling. These site-based systems have been replaced by Internet-based systems that can make thousands of calls in just a few minutes. As schools become accustomed to the mass communication services, their importance in an emergency situation or in simple weekly communications from the principal become invaluable.

For schools to fully use their budgets, districts and their schools must have a financial budget software package that permits them to track encumbered and spent amounts and to project and properly spend remaining totals. Some budget software packages include a large onetime purchase price, but almost all have an ongoing maintenance/upgrade cost associated them. It is also worthy to note that the ongoing costs for smaller districts may be larger on a per-pupil basis.

Caveats. Overall, the operating, productivity, and noninstructional software categories have some caveats. Depending on how often upgrades/refreshes become available and/or what functionality a new release of software holds, the annual allocation of $72 per student for software could be high or low. In years when the demand is not as heavy in this category, the funds could be used in any of the other categories where there is a local need or carried over for future upgrades. School budget officials must remain aware that the price for upgrades in one subcategory will cut into another subcategory when upgrades for these software products become available. Changing or upgrading any of these products usually entails temporarily hiring consultant help and providing extra and overtime hours for district and school technology-related staff.

Finally, as mentioned earlier, new computers should come with the latest operating system and productivity software used by the district, paid for from the computer hardware category. This initially saves expenditures in this software category. To also save money, districts and staff may simply postpone software upgrade cycles until the end of the useful life of a computer, using the oldest computers for more basic functions. By using these strategies, schools can spend less in this category and spend more in the computer hardware category, thus lowering the student-to-computer ratio below 3-to-1. Further, not all districts and schools use all of the software listed above, but they might have other software packages that they use to secure and regulate normal computing functions in the district. The recommended per-pupil cost figures assume that these costs will average out.

Network Equipment, Printers, and Copiers

Using a school campus size of 400 students per school as an example, the $55 per-pupil expenditure figure for this equipment category provides $22,000 per year, or $66,000 and $88,000 over three and four years, respectively. Because this category has such diverse components, it is important that districts and schools set aside the funds necessary to meet the needs of each of the components in the category: network equipment ($26), printers ($18), and copiers ($11).

Network equipment. To most district and school employees, the network equipment that provides connectivity to the district office, the Internet, and other specialized networks is invisible or transparent. Most networking equipment will have been purchased through facility funds or bond measures, as they are longer-lasting capital items. Network equipment does not need to be refreshed as often as computers, but the larger, more complex pieces of equipment should be on a maintenance contract with the manufacturer and/or include a service contract with a third-party vendor. In schools, most of this equipment will be used until it breaks or becomes obsolete.

Thus, the motivating factor for replacing network equipment usually is speed, which is measured in megabits or gigabits per second. Common networking switch speeds include 10 megabit, 100 megabit, and 1,000 megabit (commonly called gigabit). The current standard (what most schools have) is 100 megabit to desktops and 1,000 megabit on the backbone (the main lines of the network). For almost any application, this is sufficient speed within a campus. Most 10 megabit equipment is very old and should be replaced.

Over the last five years, the cost of networking equipment has dropped. A typical school of 400 students would have four to five 24-port switches ($1,300 × five 24-port switches) and a main router and core switch ($5,500), for a total of $12,000, assuming that schools have already purchased this equipment. Replacing 10 percent of the school's network equipment annually thus costs $1,200. A service contract for each piece of a school's network equipment costs about 20 percent of the original cost of the equipment or $2,400. However, most schools find it more cost-effective to contract only for the most vital network pieces and to instead purchase additional switches as replacements if they fail. This puts the site networking costs at $3,600, or $9 per pupil.

Core Internet traffic usually passes through district offices that provide filtering and other main-server services. Schools need to contribute to districts to help them offset the costs of higher-end switches and routers. An annual charge of at least $4 per pupil (totaling $1,600 in a school of 400 students) should be contributed to the district to support network switches.

As districts move to provide more access to learning materials to students, campuses should consider installing wireless access on their campus. Consumer wireless equipment is not robust enough to give secure wireless access to students. Consumer wireless equipment is difficult for technicians to monitor, can pose a security threat to networks, and can actually bring down an entire network if not configured correctly. If enterprise-level equipment is purchased and the network is designed and installed correctly, wireless access can be managed at the district office or off-site by a private company to provide safe access to all. Enterprise-level access points cost around $300 to $400 and provide a hardwired connection to tap into the network. A campus of 400 students may have four or five access points. The main cost of the wireless solution is the managing server and application, which can cost up to $20,000, depending on the size of the district. A $4 annual per-pupil expenditure is allocated to wireless costs for districts and schools to properly create secure wireless access on campuses. Once the server is purchased, more access points can be added annually to complete a network.

Creating secure wireless networks allows schools the ultimate flexibility in providing Internet access to their students. The Consortium for School Networking suggests using wireless networks to leverage student-owned computing devices such as laptops, iPads, and other devices and to effectively lower the student-to-computer ratio on a campus. Allowing students to use their own devices on campus can lower the student-to-computer ratio but will necessitate changes to school policies, which could have a large effect on school learning culture.

The wide area network (WAN) that provides the gateway to the Internet is one of the main administrative and instructional resources for educators. The data lines that compose this network must remain uncongested for teachers and administrators to maximize their efficiency. Most elementary campuses have at least one T-1 line to their site; middle and high schools commonly have two or more T-1 lines to their site. The T-1 line has a capacity of only 1.5 megabits. Many times, T-1 lines reach capacity at peak times on campuses, frustrating users. It is important for administrators, teachers, and students to understand that there is a limited amount of bandwidth and that it should be used for educational purposes. There are other types of data lines that provide higher connection speeds; however, many of these are not available in all areas and are typically higher in price.

Districts usually use E-Rate funds to offset the monthly cost of their T-1 or other data line which, before discounts, can cost approximately $250 a month (or $3,000 a year) or more. Districts then have to pay an access charge to an Internet provider to provide Internet service. This cost varies by service provider but can be estimated at around $500 per school per year. So the total school cost of linking a 400-pupil school to the Internet is $ 3,500 per year, or $ 9 per pupil.

Totaling the costs of T-1 or other data lines, an annual 10 percent replacement of network equipment, maintaining service contracts, and beginning to provide wireless access tabulates to a $26 annual per-pupil expenditure for network-related expenses.

Printers and Copiers. Computer prices listed in the computer purchase category do not include the initial costs for workstation printers, but each computer must have some method available to print. Schools now purchase higher-end, networked laser printers for each classroom instead of attaching ink-jet printers to each individual workstation (laser printers are more cost-effective). In addition to classroom printers, each school should have at least two mid-range color laser printers for the office to use for communications to community members and parents. Since most small districts do not have the in-house expertise to repair printers, contracting with an outside vendor is common practice.

The cost of an inkjet printer is a nominal $80; however, inkjet printers are more expensive to maintain as well as operate (high ink costs) and are not recommended. Prices for high-quality laser printers have dropped considerably over the last five years, making laser printers the preferred choice even at the classroom level. A quality networked black-and-white laser printer suitable for steady classroom use is $300. Color laser printers are also available for classroom use for just over $400. Considering the price difference, a color laser printer is preferred, although ongoing costs for four colors of toner and other supplies must be managed by staff at the school.

Assuming that a 400-student school contains 20 classrooms (each with one laser printer) and at least two higher-end laser printers in the office ($600 each), the initial cost per student for the printing equipment would approximate $9,200, or approximately $23 a student ($9,200/400 students). Assuming a printer life cycle of four years, the annual cost for this element is $6 per student. The real costs of printing depend on the frequency of use and the volume of printing done (cost of paper, ink, and toner). With the number of online resources increasing, teachers, students, and administrators tend to print as much as the budget can support. Assigning a cost of $12 per student annually to a 400-student campus provides the campus with an annual budget of $4,800 for supplies such as paper, toner, drum kits, etc. Thus, printers and printing costs per pupil annually would be $18. This includes all toner and paper for the office, including its administrative functions.

Depending on size, each elementary school should have a high-speed copier that can meet the demands of its teachers and other staff. Depending on their size, secondary schools may need additional copiers. Most districts maintain contracts with vendors that repair and maintain these machines. Many sign lease agreements and pay for service on a *per click* basis (*per click* meaning per page). Whether a machine is bought or leased can play a factor in the final costs. Life cycle of specific machines and the volume of copying required by leasing companies determine whether one or the other method is more cost-effective for any particular school or district. When paper, toner, service contracts, leases, and other costs are factored in, the average cost per copy approximates $.025 per copy. Assigning an $11-per-pupil-per-year cost for photocopies allows each student 440 copies a year, or approximately 50 copies a month (for a nine-month school year). This number may seem high, but as staff implements more Response to Intervention (RTI) and tries to differentiate instruction, supplemental materials outside of traditional textbooks must be used.

Instructional Software and Hardware

The $52-per-pupil figure for this technology category provides $20,800 per year for the 400-pupil school. Funds in this category should be split evenly among components until sufficient hardware has been purchased (hardware, $26; software, $26); then, as hardware needs diminish, a larger portion of the funds can be spent on instructional software that can assist in boosting achievement. These funds are very important to educators at the district and school levels, because in other states and contexts, most districts and schools run out of funds before they can purchase the instructional tools that work on technology (instead, they may only have money for purchasing the technology itself).

Of the $52 per-pupil figure earlier, $26 may be spent on instructional hardware such as LCD projectors ($500 to $700), smart boards ($3,500, depending on features), document cameras ($300), digital cameras ($200), digital video cameras ($250), and so on. This additional hardware allows teachers to bring multimedia resources alive. It also gives students the opportunity to bring their own experiences into the classroom through digital pictures and images.

When projectors, interactive whiteboards, and document cameras are installed, there will be more opportunity to use multimedia instructional software typified in student courseware and assessment packages. Reading packages such as Accelerated Reader, writing assessments such as My Access, mathematics courseware, and multimedia resources such as Discovery Education (www. discoveryeducation.com/teachers/) present digital curricular solutions. Each of these products is based on an annual subscription, which costs $5 to $17 per student for each individual package. There are also products such as Wireless Generation and Renaissance Learning's STAR Enterprise that assist teachers in formatively assessing their students and provide immediate instructive multimedia content to help reinforce instructional concepts in which students have shown weakness.

Administrative solutions that help administrators analyze test scores include products such as Edusoft. Costs of a student administration system might also be considered a part of this component. Costs of these systems vary greatly ($5 to $15 annually).

If the costs of all these instructional packages were totaled, the amount would exceed the $26 per student annually assigned to this component, but not every school will use all of these packages. Schools and districts must analyze their needs and then order those packages that target the needs of their population. They must then share their successes with neighboring schools and districts. Additionally, as mentioned previously, after all classrooms have been better equipped, funds from the hardware component of this category can be shifted to instructional software component.

Sources of Funding

In addition to state and local funds, there are two federal sources of funding for educational technology. The first is Title II D of the No Child Left Behind Act (NCLB), also known as the Enhancing Education Through Technology grant (EETT). These funds, which are distributed to state departments of education, are based on a formula that includes the number of disadvantaged students. Though the level of funding for this federal program fluctuates over time, it should be viewed as a strategic additional resource that states, districts, and schools can use for whatever specific new technology needs that may arise.

The second is the E-Rate program that helps schools connect to the Internet and build internal networks within their buildings. This program is administered by the Schools and Library Division (SLD) of the Federal Communications Commission (FCC). Districts apply directly to the federal government to participate. The assistance this program provides can be significant to a district. Since funding is substantially based on the percentage of disadvantaged students within a district, this program primarily helps districts with concentrations of students from lower-income backgrounds and offers limited participation to other, more economically advantaged districts. Nevertheless, this source of funding should be viewed as a second strategic resource to help fund the above recommendations for providing computers and related technologies.

Using Information Technologies for Instruction

Online learning is expanding at an accelerated rate across the country, and full access to online learning requires the kinds of technology costs in the above section of the chapter. This means that schools need to budget approximately $250 per pupil to maintain an updated technology base.

The International Association for K–12 Online Learning (iNACOL, see www.iNACOL.org) estimates that over 1.5 million K–12 students were engaged in online learning and blended learning during the 2009–2010 school year through multiple online learning systems, including state-supported virtual schools, multiple-district-supported virtual schools, charter schools, homeschooling, university-based programs, and blended instructional programs that are growing inside traditional public schools (iNACOL, 2010).[2] This is about a 50 percent increase from the estimated numbers for the 2007–2008 school year. The iNACOL 2010 report stated the following for the United States:

- 48 states provide supplemental or full-time online learning opportunities for at least some students in the state.
- 38 states have state-supported virtual schools or state-led online programs, with more slated to start in 2011.
- 30 states as well as Washington, D.C., have full-time online schools serving students statewide.
- 20 states provide both supplemental and full-time online learning options statewide.

The bottom line is that online learning is expanding at a fast clip around the country (and the globe) and in most instances costs less than do traditional, brick-and-mortar-school–based public school instructional programs.

These online initiatives provide a wide range of new learning opportunities, including the following:

- expanding the range of courses available to students, particularly students in small rural and inner-city schools
- providing effective teachers in subjects that have a shortage of qualified individuals
- providing credit recovery for students who are behind in acquiring the class credits needed to graduate from high school
- providing additional learning opportunities for students struggling to meet high-performance standards
- providing flexibility for students who, for any number of reasons, cannot engage in learning during traditional school times
- providing technology skills by embedding technology expertise within the instructional program
- meeting the technology needs of millennial students, who now spend much time online using computers and playing computer-based video games, and attempting to turn those skills into learning opportunities

This is not to argue that all online learning opportunities are totally effective; some are and some are less so. It is only to note that the scope of online learning and the purposes to which it is addressed are vast and, with blended learning, are entering into traditional school buildings. One long-term issue is whether online learning will be co-opted by public schools and become a high-cost addition or will be used to transform traditional schooling so that it is both more effective and less expensive, thus playing a strategic role in school redesign during tough budget times and also in the future, once budgets improve.

Most online programs can be divided into three categories: (1) those that provide supplemental courses for students enrolled in a traditional schools, (2) those that provide a full set of courses for students who are enrolled full-time in the online program, and (3) those that are being blended into traditional school programs, providing online instruction inside a brick-and-mortar school.

The remaining five parts of this section discuss the many ways that the computer technologies described in the first section of this paper are used to help deliver the instructional program. The first two parts address online instruction outside of brick-and-mortar schools, including state-supported virtual schools and K–12 programs available from private vendors, such as Advance Placement courses. The third part discusses what is now called *blended instruction*, which combines online learning with teachers inside traditional brick-and-mortar public schools. The fourth part discusses the evidence on the effectiveness of online learning, and the fifth part discusses cost issues.

Virtual Schools

State-supported virtual schools or state-initiated online learning programs are generally created by state legislation, operated by a state-level agency (usually—but not always—the state department of education), and funded by a state appropriation or grant for the purpose of providing online learning opportunities for students across the state. State-supported virtual schools provide fully for online courses, including the course content, a teacher, and a learning management system, whereas state-initiated online programs provide online content or resources to schools. Most state-supported virtual schools are primarily supplemental; they provide multiple course opportunities that supplement student learning in brick-and-mortar schools. Full-time online schools, by contrast, are the main and only providers of education for their students and primarily exist in charter schools, though are growing via state-supported virtual schools as well.

As of the 2009–2010 school year, most state-supported virtual schools had a small number of course enrollments (4,000 to 16,000 students, with one student in each semester course), received funding from a state appropriation, provided courses primarily for middle school and high school students (though mainly high school), and were run by a state agency, with accountability for student performance lodged in the district where the student attended school for most courses. On the other hand, Florida's virtual school, the largest in the country, had nearly 215,000 course enrollments in 2010; provided programs for elementary school, middle school, and high school students; allowed some students to attend full-time if they wanted; and let the student carry his or her state funding to the virtual school. Further, as state-supported virtual schools expand and have more full-time students, some states are allowing private sector companies (such as K12 Inc. and Connections Academy) to run them, just as is the case with many charter virtual schools that offer full-time online programming for students enrolled in them.

Over 30 states have a virtual school, all of which, in 2011, were in a state of flux caused in part by funding challenges (as a result of the national recession) as well as expanding possibilities for and interest in online learning. The following section profiles a variety of state-supported virtual schools in Florida, North Carolina, Georgia, and Wisconsin.

Florida Virtual School (FLVS). The Florida Virtual School started operations in 1997 as a supplemental program for students in Grades 6–12. By the end of the 2007–2008 school year, it was providing services to over 60,000 K–12 students (Means, Toyama, Murphy, Bakia, & Jones, 2009). The elementary school offering is delivered via partnership with Connections Academy. Two short years later, that number approached 100,000 students, and the number of courses taken exceeded 200,000 (Watson, Murin, Vashaw, Gemin, & Rapp, 2010). This growth was aided by legislation requiring all Florida students to take at least one online course prior to graduation (Watson et. al, 2010). Florida Virtual School courses are also available for a fee to non-Florida residents. FLVS offers in excess of 100 courses online, including AP courses (Staker, 2011).

In addition to offering courses directly, Florida Virtual School also acts as a franchisor for course delivery. As of Fall 2010, 39 Florida school districts acted as franchises of Florida Virtual School, delivering almost 18,000 course enrollments to middle school and high school students. This franchising strategy extended the reach of the Florida Virtual School beyond traditional public schools to include homeschooled children as well as those attending private schools (Watson et al., 2010).

All instructional staff must be state certified and all instructional content must meet state standards. Florida Virtual School students are required to take part in all statewide assessments and are subject to the same accountability measures as brick-and-mortar schools.

As of the 2009–2010 school year, the Florida Virtual School employed 898 full-time teachers and 55 part-time teachers (Watson et al., 2010). The average class size is roughly 25 students, and the student-to-teacher ratio is approximately 150-to-1 (Staker, 2011).

Per-student funding for the 2009–2010 school year was $469 per semester course. Total funding was $101.3 million. Per-student funding for the 2010–2011 school year was expected to drop to $432 per semester course, while total funding should reach $116.7 million (Watson et al., 2010). Note that if the per-pupil per-semester course figure were inflated to $500, the cost would be $6,000 per student for 6 year-long or 12 semester courses, much lower than a traditional district-run school.

North Carolina Virtual Public School (NCVPS). NCVPS was created by the North Carolina State Board of Education in 2005. All entities that wish to offer e-learning opportunities and receive state funding must first seek approval from NCVPS (Watson et al., 2010). Thus, North Carolina Virtual Public School serves as the de jure clearinghouse for all virtual public school instruction. The North Carolina Virtual School delivered its first e-learning solution in the summer of 2007. For the 2009–2010 school year, the North Carolina Virtual School had 73,658 enrollments for Grades 9–12 and boasted an annualized growth rate of over 300 percent (Watson et al., 2010).

Current legislation constrains the courses offered to Grades 9–12 and does not permit physical education to be taught online. Dual enrollments (e.g. college and high school) are permitted under the current law, and there were 11,000 such enrollments during the 2009–2010 school year (Watson et al., 2010).

The North Carolina Virtual School is funded based on a combination of prior-year enrollments and projected growth rates. Monies are then transferred from the public school districts to NCVPS based upon the expected enrollments. For the 2010–2011 school year, NCVPS had an estimated budget of $20 million, which would fund 46,000 single-credit course enrollments (this cap will likely be expanded through legislative action). This translates to $435 per credit course enrolled. Dollars must be allocated with 85 percent to teacher pay and 15 percent to operations (Watson et al., 2010).

Georgia Virtual School. The Georgia Virtual School (GAVS) was created legislatively in 2005 and became operational under a ruling by the State Board of Education in 2006. During the 2009–2010 school year, the Georgia Virtual School delivered instructional services to 5,000 full-time students and 14,000 supplemental-education students in middle school and high school. Supplemental course enrollment has grown by roughly 40 percent over the last three years.

The Georgia Virtual School has also served as a provider of credit recovery course work. For the 2009–2010 school year, there were just shy of 6,700 enrollments for this self-paced, computer-led program. Students recover credits in previously failed or uncompleted courses by taking and passing end-of-unit exams. The minimum passing score is 85 percent. Scores below 85 percent trigger a complete unit review and a second test, which requires a score of 70 percent or higher to move on to the next unit. Between 70 and 80 percent of students who participate in the credit recovery program successfully recover these credits (Watson et al., 2010).

Wisconsin Virtual School. The Wisconsin Virtual School (WVS) was sanctioned and put into operation in 2000. The Wisconsin Virtual School (also known as Wisconsin's Web Academy or WWA) serves Grades 6–12, offering a suite of over 170 courses. The Wisconsin Virtual School administered over 2,200 course enrollments during the 2009–2010 school year, a 26 percent increase over prior year. Currently, Wisconsin caps the number of online students at 5,350, but this number is in flux as of August 2011, due to pending legislation and legal challenges.

State licensure is required for online instructors (there is a home-schooling exemption, however), and online teachers must complete a 30-hour professional development course in addition to the regular licensing procedure.

K–12 Programs From Private Companies

Simultaneous with the development of state-supported virtual schools and charter virtual schools has been the emergence of online learning opportunities provided by many private sector companies—Advanced Academics, Connections Academy, Insight Schools, and K12 Inc. to name a few. These companies offer online (meaning the student simply needs a computer connected to the Internet) the full range of curriculum from kindergarten through Grade 12, teachers who are available online for instruction and support, and a learning management system (course tests, records of assignments completed, etc.). As noted above, some state-supported virtual schools have contracted with such companies to run their virtual school for full-time students; many charter schools around the country have done the same. The following profiles two of the most popular systems offering full-time online schools—Connections Academy and K12 Inc.—as well as the online offerings of the Edison Learning and Advanced Placement courses, nearly all of which are now offered in an online format.

Connections Academy. Connections Academy (CA) specializes in the development of virtual charter schools that serve full-time online students. CA commenced operations in 2002, with a two-state offering. Currently CA offers instruction in 23 schools across several states. Its curriculum spans the K–12 spectrum, although not all grades may be served in all states. Additionally, CA offers a national tuition-based virtual school for all grades, with tuition costs ranging from approximately $5,000 to $6,000 per academic year, depending on grade.

Connection Academy's business model can best be described as an in-home public school. Their solution set encompasses not just courses and coursework but also the opportunity to join clubs and virtual organizations, to enhance the student experience beyond just academics. In addition to offering these turnkey solutions for the homeschooling market and virtual charter school market, Connections Academy also operates private K–12 online schools through its National Connections Academy (NaCA) arm, headquartered in Baltimore, Maryland. NaCA had a total nationwide student enrollment in excess of 1,500 for the 2009–2010 school year. As contrasted with the CA offering, NaCA also allows part-time registration.

K12 Inc. K12 Inc. was established in 1999. It offers a suite of online learning solutions across the entire K–12 spectrum. Solutions range from a turnkey virtual public school at the high end to individual coursework for other grades. Parents can purchase K12 Inc.'s online program to facilitate homeschooling or as a supplement to a student's brick-and-mortar education.

Though the instructional focus is online, all courses also include extensive supplementary material as well as textbooks, reference materials, lesson guides, and necessary materials such as art supplies or scientific equipment. Lessons are self-paced.

The proprietary curricular offering covers all K–8 core courses (English and language arts, mathematics, science, history, art and music, and world languages) and complies with current state standards. Additionally, a remedial literacy program is available for struggling readers in Grades 3–5. The high school offering includes over 150 core courses from remedial to AP classes that are developed in-house. Elective courses, however, are licensed from third parties and distributed through K12 Inc., which also offers a management information systems module to handle administrative tasks such as course enrollment, grading, and transcript generation.

According to the K12 Inc. website, course pricing is highly variable depending upon whether the instruction is teacher aided, if supplemental materials are being used, how many courses are being bought, how many students are enrolled at one time, and whether the courses are for Grades K–5, 6–8, or 9–12 (see www.k12.com/enroll-or-buy/course-pricing). For example, a teacher-supported five-course high school year would run $4,250 for non-AP courses; AP classes require an additional $50 per-pupil per-semester premium. Lab courses such as chemistry or biology would add another $353 per year per course to cover materials. For elementary school, a teacher-supported five-course year would run $2,750 plus materials of roughly $50 to $100 per course, bringing the expected total to around $3,500 per year.

Edison Learning. Edison Learning, (formerly Edison Schools) was established in 1992. Edison Learning is a for-profit full-service provider of education solutions; the organization operates in the United States, the United Kingdom, and Saudi Arabia. Enrollments across all Edison Learning sites in all countries exceed 450,000.

Edison Learning offerings run the gamut from tailored interventions for all kinds of students to school turnaround to new school start-up. Edison Learning works in partnership with local authorities to develop tailored education solutions. For example, eCourses are constituted as modular online courses to permit the matching of high school student needs with the necessary amount of online instruction, while eAcademy serves as a framework that can be filled in by the local district with turnkey offerings the district deems optimal for its student body. Delivery mechanisms range from traditional models of classroom instruction (at its eight drop-in credit recovery centers in Ohio, which opened in 2010 and 2011) to blended online instruction (used in its turnaround school projects).

Edison Learning costs are quite variable, as their offerings run from single courses to entire school programs.

Advanced Placement. As should be clear, nearly all Advanced Placement courses are now available in multiple online formats from multiple online providers (including state virtual schools, such as the Florida Virtual School) to course offerings from private online companies (such as Edison Learning, Connections Academy, and K12 Inc.).

Blended Instructional Programs

Blended learning is an educational practice that combines online learning and brick-and-mortar teaching and learning and is a fast-growing phenomenon in education (Horn & Staker, 2011).

As such, it combines two modes of delivering instruction: online and face-to-face.

The simple presence of those two modes, while necessary, is not in and of itself sufficient. First, the face-to-face mode must offer supervised learning by a qualified individual at a facility adapted for that purpose. Second, students must be able to exercise a degree of control over the frequency, form, ordering, and time of instructional delivery. These two requirements are essential.

Blended learning can alter the role of the teacher from one of a content deliverer to one of a coach and can expand learning opportunities by making them available anytime and anyplace, in addition to what is available inside the school building. In some respects, blended learning can be a catchall term for a number of different modalities. For example, the Innosight Institutes has identified six distinct models that could all be considered variations on blended learning. These models range from the classic brick-and-mortar school in which online learning is strictly supplemental to a flexible model where the relative dosages of face-to-face and online instruction are dictated by student learning needs to a fully online model where students work at a remote site and face-to-face interactions are employed on an as-needed basis (Staker, 2011).

This fluid nature of blended learning can leave it vulnerable to being repurposed for uses other than those originally intended. For example, online learning advocates argue that blended learning can either be co-opted by the public schools, becoming an add-on—and additional cost—to traditional education, or used to transform education to something that has students inside a building for most of the day but with online instruction comprising most of the instruction, thus allowing schools to have fewer teachers, who play different, more facilitative roles.

The following profiles the blended learning programs offered by the Rocketship Education School in San Jose and the School of One in New York City.

Rocketship Education. Rocketship Education was founded in 2006 as a nonprofit charter management organization. Rocketship's target population is urban, low-income elementary school students. As of 2010, there were three San Jose, CA elementary schools in the fleet.

Rocketship employs a blended model comprised of 75 percent classroom instruction and 25 percent online learning (Staker, 2011). Daily classroom instruction consists of two blocks of literacy/social studies and one block of math/science. The online portion of instruction takes the form of a Learning Lab block designed to complement classroom instruction. The Learning Lab is a separate room where students are sent to build competencies in specific areas of need (updated daily) as well as polish more general skills (Staker, 2011). The room is supervised by a noncredentialed observer. Rocketship does not use curriculum programs created by the company but instead chooses from among a number of reading and mathematics content providers.

The combination of blended learning with the use of nontraditional staff allows Rocketship to deploy resources efficiently. Classroom instruction boasts a 23-to-1 student-to-teacher ratio, while the overall student-teacher ratio (when the Learning Lab is included) is 31-to-1. This staffing model frees up around $500,000 per year, which Rocketship invests in things like 20 percent higher teacher salaries, a Response to Intervention program, professional development, and academic deans (Staker, 2011).

Academic results appear strong for one of the first Rocketship schools—Mateo Sheedy Elementary School in San Jose; this school was first in the California accountability Academic Performance Index (API) rankings (925) in Santa Clara County and fifth in California among similar schools; Si Se Puede elementary school in the same community ranked second and fifteenth, respectively with an API ranking of 886 (Staker, 2011).

School of One. New York City's School of One is a flexible form of blended learning. The basic idea is to provide the student with a learning environment and instruction tailored to individual needs. School of One was launched in 2009 as a pilot and is initially focused on delivering middle school math instruction.

Students attend a traditional brick-and-mortar school, but that is where the traditional model stops. Students log on to a computer as soon as they enter the school and are given their individual lesson plan (called a *playlist*) for the day. Playlists are created in response to the need for students to learn specific content, but the exercises are not necessarily completed on a computer. Instead, they take whatever form best suits the students (e.g., small-group work, individual assignments worked on at the whiteboard, etc.).

Learning style and content area needs are assessed via diagnostic tests. The test results are sent to the central office where the initial playlist is then created and sent back to the student's teacher. The teacher reviews the playlist, modifies it if needed, and then distributes it to the student's desktop. Students work through the playlist during the school day and are given a brief diagnostic quiz at the end of the day to assess whether they can move on to the next topic or need a review. Initial results appear positive. A recent school system audit showed that students achieved a 28 percent gain on their end-of-program diagnostic tests.

At this point, costs are as high as or higher than those in a tradition school. For the 2009 version of School of One, a team of four teachers, four graduate students, and two high school interns were required to service a group of 80 middle school students.

Effectiveness of Online Learning

Technology has the potential to increase student achievement when teachers use instructionally sound techniques that take advantage of effective pedagogy and are linked to a rigorous core curriculum program. In cases in which old pedagogy is transferred to a new electronic medium, results are mixed (Archer, 2000; Earle, 2002; Kulik, 1994, 2003). As the previous paragraphs suggest, although there is great potential for technology to enhance learning, the ability to do so rests on the soundness of the core curriculum and how technologies are used to provide instruction (Clarke & Estes, 1999).

It also is difficult to compare impacts across all kinds of online learning; some programs are geared to credit recovery, serving students who are below-average achievers, while others provide the full curriculum online and cater to more-motivated, high-achieving students who also benefit from high levels of parental involvement and oversight. Nevertheless, there is insufficient but growing evidence on the impact of online learning. Further, many—but not all—of the studies have been conducted on students older than those in K–12 schools, so caution must be taken in reviewing results. For example, in 2009, the U.S. Department of Education sponsored a meta-analysis of 51 studies of online learning and concluded that online instruction was at least as effective as traditional face-to-face instruction (Means et al., 2009). That analysis drew two major conclusions:

1. Students who took all or part of a class online did better, on average, than students who took the same course through traditional face-to-face instruction.

2. Instruction that combined online and face-to-face instruction had relatively larger positive impacts on student learning than either only face-to-face instruction or only online instruction.

Many programs and schools collect and publish other indicators of impact, such as course completion, persistence in school, and so on. The iNACOL (2010) report showed that three virtual school programs—Apex Learning, the Florida Virtual School, and the Virtual High School—all had Advanced Placement examination pass rates higher than the national average of 60 percent.

The success of the Rocketship Education, a blended learning program in a high-poverty, high-minority elementary school in San Jose (Davis, 2011), is testimony to the potential effectiveness of online learning for elementary students from lower-income, minority, and non-English-speaking backgrounds.

Clearly, more research on the impact of good online instruction is needed. But evidence to date suggests that these approaches—which are quite varied—can be at least as effective as face-to-face instruction in traditional schools when paired with the appropriate student population. Further, multiple online and computer-based instructional programs have also proved effective for students with special needs (*Education Week*, 2011). Since online learning is more aligned with the technology revolution impacting the world of work and leisure, it should be investigated thoroughly and seriously by all schools especially in these tight fiscal times, because as this chapter shows, its costs also appear lower than those of traditional schools.

Costs of Online Learning

It is hard to generalize about the costs of online learning. There needs to be about $250 per pupil for the basic computer technologies, but since the systems for online learning vary so dramatically, no one cost can be determined for all programs. Full-time online learning programs will cost more than supplemental programs. Programs that create their own courses will have larger up-front costs but lower operating costs; programs that license course content will have somewhat higher ongoing costs.

Nevertheless, emerging evidence suggests that as a whole, online learning costs much less than traditional face-to-face instruction. Though an early study of the costs of virtual schools concluded that they cost about the same as brick-and-mortar schools (Anderson, Augenblick, DeCesare, & Conrad, 2006), that conclusion should be viewed with skepticism today. First, most virtual schools have no brick-and-mortar costs. Second, they usually also have a much larger student-teacher ratio and thus have lower teachers costs as well as lower (if any) administrative costs, both of which can significantly reduce total costs.

Third, most studies show that virtual schools and online learning cost less than traditional schooling:

- A 2005 legislative study in Ohio analyzed the costs of five statewide online schools and found that they cost $5,382 per student, compared to $7,452 for students in brick-and-mortar charter schools and $8,437 for students in traditional, non-charter schools. Technology comprised 28 percent of the spending in the virtual schools (a significantly higher percentage than in brick-and-mortar schools), followed by instruction staff at 23 percent, administration at 1 percent, and curriculum at 9 percent (Ohio Legislative Committee on Education Oversight, 2005).

- A 2008 survey of 20 directors of full-time virtual schools identified an average yearly cost for a full-time online student at $4,310, compared to the 2006–2007 national average spending of $9,683 per pupil (Cavanaugh, 2009).

- The Alliance for Excellent Education reported that Wisconsin virtual schools operated on a budget of about $6,500 per pupil, compared to the 2009 national average of almost $10,000 per pupil for traditional schools (Wise & Rothman, 2010). Indeed, several district-sponsored virtual charter schools in Wisconsin earned the district close to $10,000 in state aid but required a payment of only $5,000 to $6,000 to a charter company (such as K12 Inc.) to run their virtual program, thus earning the district a profit on each virtual charter school student.

- Connections Academy charges just $5,000 to $6,000 per pupil for a full-time student enrollment in a virtual school.

- The Florida Virtual School costs just under $500 per pupil per semester course, which totals just $6,000 per year for a full array of 12 semester courses.

- K12 Inc. costs range from about $3,500 to $4,000 per pupil for a full elementary program to about $6,000 per pupil for the high school program, and a bit more if the high school program includes more lab science courses or AP courses.

In sum, it seems that approximately $6,000 to $7,000 per pupil is a good upward-bound estimate of what full-time online programs cost today, with per-course per-pupil costs in the $500 to $600 range for students taking just one course for either credit recovery or Advanced Placement.

It seems reasonable to conclude that full-time virtual schools, most of which provide some level of teacher support in an online format, cost significantly less than traditional public schools. As a result, online programming should be on the strategic planning agenda for all districts and schools in these times of fiscal constraint and uncertain education budgets. Further, online programming allows all high schools in the country—regardless of location and fiscal condition—to offer Advanced Placement courses at costs far less than hiring additional teachers to provide face-to-face instruction to small numbers of students, especially in rural areas.

Indeed, the multiplicity of online programming means that virtually any school can offer low-demand courses at low costs, certainly at costs far less than providing a full-time teacher to a tiny group of students. Online learning also means that students for a course do not have to come from just one school or even a single geographic area; the pool of students can be aggregated across the state or even country to make the provision of the course cost-effective.

States and districts must continue to work on how funding for online education can be blended with traditional school funding. Most state virtual schools are add-on programs, costing above what is given to traditional public schools; is there a way to have the dollars provided to traditional public schools follow the child when they take online courses or switch to a full-time online program? Is it right for districts to make a profit on students who generate full state funding (of say, $10,000 per pupil) but attend lower-cost virtual schools that cost thousands of dollars less? Conversely, is it appropriate for states to provide less funding to virtual schools than even their lowered costs, as often is the case? And over time, how can the economies of virtual schools be captured by states and districts so all students have the best education and the appropriate mix of online and face-to-face instruction, both appropriately funded?

Summary

Online learning is growing at an accelerated across America's schools.

- More and more students are enrolled full-time in virtual schools, whether operated by state agencies or charter schools, and even more are taking some courses online.
- Each year, more states require students to take some courses online as a condition for high school graduation.
- Moreover, research finds that most students do better or as well with online learning as compared to traditional schooling
- It also seems that a combination of online and face-to-face learning is better than either face-to-face or online learning alone.
- Blended learning, an approach for using online technologies within the regular classroom, taps this potential of doing both.

To support student access to the Internet and such online learning, schools and districts need to allocate about $250 per pupil annually for hardware, software, networking, and instructional technology, which is about 2.5 percent of an average budget of $10,000 per student. Moreover, nearly all virtual schools cost significantly less than traditional public schooling, with results no worse than traditional schools.

In these times of tight budgets, the potential of computer technologies to both enhance learning and reduce costs should be tapped by every education leader in the country. It is not often that an organization can do more with less, but it seems technology-based education has matured sufficiently to make that possibility a reality in education.

Indeed, it seems that approximately $6,000 to $7,000 per pupil is a good upward-bound estimate of what full-time online programs cost today, compared to $10,000+ for traditional schooling, with per-course per-pupil costs in the $500-to-$600 range for students taking just one course either for initial credit or for credit recovery, even including Advanced Placement courses.

The country's education system should not just make online learning an add-on and added cost to traditional schooling but should use the power of online learning and blended education to boost student achievement and simultaneously lower education costs or run education programs with reduced budgets but increased student performance.

Notes

1. This section draws heavily from Price, Odden, and Picus (2010).
2. These numbers are probably lower-bound underestimates of students involved in online learning, as many students taking courses in traditional schools might not be counted in these estimates.

6

When Budget Cuts Are Necessary

- The Center on Education Policy reported in the summer of 2011 that fully 70 percent of school districts experienced funding cuts during the 2010–2011 school year, and over 80 percent predicted spending cuts for the 2011–2012 school year.
- The lead article in *Education Week*'s back-to-school issue in late August 2011 was titled "Districts Face Painful Cuts as School Year Begins."
- Sam Dillon (2011), the education reporter for the *New York Times,* wrote in July 2011 about how instructional time was being cut across the country as states and districts reduced the school year and cut extended-day and summer school programs in response to budget shortfalls, acts that will blunt efforts to improve student learning.

The fact is that dealing with budget cuts is *the* school district reality for the near future.

This chapter shows how districts and schools can bring together all the ideas outlined in the previous chapters and engage in a strategic budget-cutting process in ways that retain progress toward boosting student learning. In other words, this chapter addresses the admittedly unattractive challenge of what to do if, after resource reallocation, restructuring school programs, and implementing every possible efficiency, budget cuts are still needed. The goal of this chapter is to suggest budget cuts that will not negatively impact the core instructional program, will provide at least some extra help for struggling students, and will simultaneously improve both the effectiveness and efficiency of the available education dollars.

The chapter first identifies the goals and principles that should drive budget cutbacks as well as any kind of resource reallocation. It then reviews educator talent issues—including such issues as salary freezes, new recruitment strategies, dismissing by effectiveness, contributions to health and pension benefits, and new salary structures—that should be on the table at all times but particularly when budget cuts are necessary. The last section of the chapter goes through strategic budget-cutting exercises for three types of schools—a well-funded elementary school, a slimly funded high school, and an average-funded middle school—showing how such issues as being flexible with class size, looking hard at school schedules, insuring rigor and effectiveness for core instruction, and providing for some highly effective extra help for struggling students (in addition to special education and English as a second language [ESL] services) can all be part of effective resource allocation, even if the budget needs to be cut. This section also reiterates the potential of online learning to boost performance and reduce costs, a reality that needs to be considered in these tough fiscal times.

Cost Pressures, Goals, and Principles to Guide Strategic Budgeting

As argued in Chapter 3, schools first need to be aware of the cost pressures the public places on them to reduce class size, enhance electives, and continuously provide compensation increases, despite the budget context. As stated in that chapter, positively responding to these cost pressures consumes dollars, does little to help the bottom line of improved student learning, and exacerbates the fiscal plight of schools when dollars are tight. To resist these cost pressures, school and district leaders need political support not only from school board members but also from the broader political community, as education leaders will be pushing against what the public wants and trying to align resources with strategies to boost student performance—for which there is less intense public clamor.

So Step 1 in strategic budgeting is recognizing and (to the degree possible) resisting the cost pressures that continuously bear down on the education system and make strategic budgeting harder.

Step 2 then is to scrutinize the budget in a very strategic way. To do that, this book argues that the task is to link scarce resources to those strategies most likely to boost student achievement. To make those links strategically, schools and districts need the following:

- clear goals
- a programmatic Plan of Action to achieve those goals
- an human resource strategy designed to acquire the teachers and administrators needed to implement the Plan of Action
- clear understanding of the core resource needs of that Plan of Action
- a set of principles to help determine the priorities for aligning the resources schools have to the core resource needs of their Plan of Action

To reiterate, the goals driving the recommendations and points made in this book are student achievement in core academic subjects—mathematics, science, English/reading/language arts/writing, and history. Each district and every school needs specific, ambitious, and numerical goals for increasing student achievement in these core academic areas. Without such goals, it is impossible to make tough budget decisions about which programs and strategies have priority over another.

The next element for strategic budgeting is for a school and district to have a specific Plan of Action, a set of programs and strategies it has decided will help it to dramatically improve student academic achievement. Chapter 1 describes the Plan of Action undergirding this book; Chapter 1 argued that this plan has worked all across the country, in small, medium, and large schools; in rich and poor schools; and in urban, rural, and suburban communities and has multiple randomized trial studies bolstering each individual strategy and the combined strategies in a schoolwide effort.

A third element for strategic budgeting is to know the resource needs of every element of the Plan of Action—otherwise school and district leaders will not be able to address budget issues in specific and concrete ways. Chapter 2 identified the specific resource needs of this book's Plan of Action.

A related aspect of knowing the resource needs of every element of the Plan of Action is to be able to set some priorities for the various elements of the Plan of Action, identifying some as absolutely core, others that should be added as the budget allows, and others that, while important and part of the overall Plan of Action, can be put at the end of the budget line when resources are limited—as is the case today—and tough budget decisions must be made.

The strategic budgeting task for schools with inadequate resources is to fund as much of the Plan of Action as is possible and to use the following six macro-principles as a guide for where and how to cut funding to meet budget realities:

1. Use these staffing recommendations as a general guideline and reallocate current staff to these configurations.

2. Be flexible about class size.

3. Do everything possible to make Tier 1 instruction—the core program—as effective as possible.

4. Organize schools so that all key teacher groups have at least three 45-minute periods a week for collaborative work (even if it means increasing in class sizes) and have at least some instructional coaching available to work with these teams.

5. Provide all of the resources to help teachers and students—especially instructional coaches and staff for extra help strategies—by varying class size. If necessary, allow class size in secondary schools to rise substantially before reducing the instructional coach and extra help staff.

6. If increasing class size still does not allow the school to fund all the needed staff, then reductions in instructional coaching, extended-day and summer school programs, and (lastly) tutoring staff should be considered.

These macro-principles for resource allocation have emerged from my experiences working with my colleague, Lawrence O. Picus, as we helped teachers and administrators all over country who have had to reduce budgets and simultaneously improve student performance. Chapter 3 provided overviews of many of the issues that need to be addressed, and the third section of this chapter shows how these budget principles can play out in different schools in different fiscal situations.

But before getting into the messy business of cutting programs and staff, schools and districts need to assess the situation with respect to their teacher and principal talent on a more general and strategic level, a topic addressed in the next section.

Ensuring a Solid Talent Foundation in Tight Fiscal Times

Chapter 4 (on educator talent) identified several initiatives districts and schools, especially urban districts, can take to increase the talent level and effectiveness of all their teachers and school leaders. The chapter also argued that many of these general human resource (HR) management initiatives would be cost-effective in the short as well as the long run. Eight major overall HR initiatives should launched by all districts but particularly in these times, when dollars are scarce and districts want every dollar spent on staff to be spent as effectively as possible:

1.   Create and use measures that indicate both teacher and principal effectiveness. Use these effectiveness measures to conduct a teacher and principal effectiveness audit of all staff in the district. Use the audit results for all key HR decisions (including moving teachers and principals across schools) to ensure a fair distribution of effective teachers and administrators as the foundation for all other staffing changes.

2.   Review the major supplier organizations of teacher and principal talent, which for many urban districts have been low-quality schools of education in low-quality institutions of higher education. Reduce teacher and principal intake from these organizations and increase hiring from places that produce better talent. If not already doing so, urban districts should consider partnering with such national talent organizations as Teach For America (TFA) and The New Teacher Project, both of which recruit, place, and train new teachers at a cost below that of any district. Further, recent research suggests that TFA recruits have a higher retention rate in the first two years than new teachers from typical teacher training colleges (Teach For America, 2010) and, as Chapter 4 documented, are more effective than are teachers from other sources. If formal partnering is not possible, districts should also review and perhaps use the selection criteria TFA uses to select individuals into that program; recent research suggests that those criteria are linked to greater teacher effectiveness during subsequent years of teaching (Dobbie, 2011).

3.   Use effectiveness indicators to make tenure decisions about teachers and principals; take every action possible to make sure that only effective teachers and principals are given tenure from this point on. If possible, push out the tenure decision to a teacher's fourth, fifth, or sixth year in teaching, so more and more stable evidence is available for making that important decision.

4.   Use effectiveness indicators as core parts of teacher and principal evaluations. If the results show that teacher or principal performance falls below an acceptable effectiveness level, provide assistance to help them improve performance, but if performance does not increase, use the results as a basis for dismissal.

5.   Redesign teacher and principal salary schedules to provide the major annual pay increases on the basis of effectiveness indicators, and

not years of experience or educational degrees, thus over time aligning salary levels to effectiveness levels.

6. If staff cuts need to be made in any area, use effectiveness measures to cut the most ineffective individuals first. This type of process is far superior to simply using attrition, retirements, seniority, or anything else not related to effectiveness when staff cuts must be made. As Chapter 4 documented, this will require fewer staff cuts and produce an overall more effective talent pool in place.

7. If states and districts have not already done so, it is time for educators to pay a fair share of their health and pension benefits. In many places, they already do. But the country does not need another fight like those that occurred in Wisconsin and Ohio in 2011; educators, like nearly all private and increasing numbers of public employees, should be willing to pay a portion of pension and health benefit costs.

8. Finally, take a step back and provide annual pay increases *only* when there is a budget to do so. When money is tight, especially when next year's budget is smaller than this year's budget, automatic pay increases simply exacerbate budget problems. Though I have argued that overall teacher salaries need to be raised (Odden, 2008b), raising salaries when the money is not there is poor management and places adults above kids in terms of budget priorities, which is not in line with the goal of increased student performance levels.

As Chapter 4 argued, a salary increase budget should be identified each year, and priorities for salary increases should be set; for example, first pay increases for moving from one effectiveness category to a higher category, then pay increases for teachers for subject shortages or high-need schools, then pay increases for performance bonuses, and then pay increases for years of experience—or some similar set of priorities.

Moreover, when funding is tight and especially when next year's funding is the same or less than this year's funding, salary freezes should also be in order—not just salary schedule freezes but actual salary increases, so no step and lane increases either. I have worked with more than one district facing a budget crunch and each one ignored the idea of a salary freeze. ("Oh, we can't do that, because it is negotiated." "A salary freeze is off the table.")

Wisconsin provides another example of questionable management behavior. For several years, school districts lived under what was called the Qualified Economic Offer, or QEO. If, during collective bargaining over salaries, school districts offered a 3.8 percent increase in salary and benefits, termed the QEO, then the bargaining was essentially over and the QEO determined the level of compensation increase for next year. To be sure, that produced a meager salary increase, because in most districts, health benefits consumed most of that increase, so salaries did not rise much per se. But the QEO became the automatic minimum compensation increase every year.

However, school districts also faced a revenue increase limit, which (though varied) was around 2 percent for many years. So every year those districts provided compensation increases of 3.8 percent, it far exceeded their ability to fund it with the 2 percent revenue increase constraint; so they had to cut programs for students every year. To be sure, districts that tried to provide a compensation increase less than 3.8 percent were constrained by arbitration proceedings that often required them to do so. But what emerged was almost an annual automatic compensation increase that could not be afforded and required cuts in programs for students year after year. This is not the way to run a performance-focused organization, educational or otherwise.

Most salary schedules are negotiated, and there is a contract, but when money is as tight as it has been during the past few years (and as it is likely to be for the next few years), contracts for automatic pay hikes need to be revisited. For example, when the 2011-elected mayor of Chicago, Rahm Emmanuel, learned that the educator contract in Chicago called for a 4 percent salary increase for 2011–2012, when the budget had to be cut by hundreds of millions of dollars, he announced that the city would not pay the increase. It was a tough but sound managerial decision. Paying the increases, even if deserved and negotiated, simply would have meant cutting more programs for the students.

Again, I am making the point about salary freezes only because it seems not to have been on the table in too many districts when, given the recent shortage of education dollars, salary freezes should have been one of the first steps considered. Medium- to long-term teacher salaries must be raised, especially for the more effective teachers and administrators, but in the short term, when there is no money to do so, automatic annual pay raises should be taken off the table and salary freezes made the norm, with increases provided only when money is there to do so.

The goal here is to launch a series of interlinked HR initiatives to create a foundation to insure that over time, all teachers and principals meet rigorous effectiveness standards; that promotions, pay increases, and dismissals are based on effectiveness criteria; and that automatic annual salary increases are stopped during these times when budgets are stuck or even falling. Such moves can be especially important in tight budget times, but are important strategically for sound HR management whatever the particular budget situation (Odden, 2011a).

Engaging in Strategic Budgeting

Strategic budgeting is generally the process of aligning whatever resources exist to programs and strategies that lead to improved student performance, specifically increases in student academic achievement in core subject areas. In this section, the book takes readers through a series of decisions for three different kinds of schools facing tight budgets—a well-funded elementary school, an underfunded high school, and a modestly or average-funded middle school. These scenarios supplement the middle school example that was discussed in Chapter 3.

The discussion centers around two tables, both of which are printouts from a school redesign and resource reallocation tool (http://cpre .wceruw.org/finance/redesign/schoolinfo.asp). This tool is available online for anyone who wants to use it. The tool produces two tables: one showing the school's current budget and a second showing the total costs for the staffing allocations and resources needed to fund the Plan of Action discussed in Chapter 1 using the formulas discussed in Chapter 2. Thus, the second table shows whether the school can afford all the resources required to implement an ambitious and comprehensive Plan of Action. The two tables together, therefore, show whether the school starts in a position of having more or less than the resources needed to fund the full Plan of Action.

A Well-Resourced Elementary School

Table 6.1 shows what would be considered a well-resourced elementary school. Excluding maintenance and operations, transportation, and food services, Table 6.1 shows that the total budget for this elementary school is over $5 million, making the point that elementary schools of 600 students are multimillion-dollar operations. Let's assume that the task for this school is to cut the budget by 10 percent, a result of declines in state funding as well as drops in local dollars due to lower assessed property values that have resulted in the wake of the housing downturn that started in 2006.

The school has a principal and two assistant principals—perhaps more than most elementary schools of this size (at least in schools in the South and the West). The school has no instructional support staff or coaches.

Table 6.1 Well-Resourced Elementary School: Current Resources

Title	Positions (FTE)	Revenue Per Position	Total Revenues
Principal	1	$110,000	$110,000
Assistant principals	2	$85,000	$170,000
Instructional support staff	0	$70,000	$0
Classroom teachers	33	$70,000	$2,310,000
Elective and specialist teachers	9	$70,000	$630,000
Categorical program teachers for mild special education, compensatory education, ESL, gifted and talented, etc.	8	$70,000	$560,000
Counselors	2	$70,000	$140,000
Other pupil support staff	5	$70,000	$350,000
Instructional aides	20	$23,000	$460,000
Supervisory aides	3	$20,000	$60,000
Librarians	2	$70,000	$140,000
Secretary/clerk	3	$30,000	$90,000

Discretionary Funds			
Professional development			$50,000
Equipment and technology			$150,000
Instructional materials			$84,000
Gifted and talented education			$20,000
Total of other discretionary funds			$0
Total Actual School Revenues			**$5,324,000**

ELL = English language learners
ESL = English as a second language
FTE = full-time equivalent

This elementary school has a total of 59 professional teacher positions, which includes 33 regular classroom teachers—teachers who provide instruction in grade-level classes. Dividing the number of pupils (600) by 33 produces an average class size of just over 18 (my budget-cutting mind is now thinking that a rise of just two students to 20 in each class could free up three teaching positions or a total of $210,000, with average teacher salary and benefits being $70,000).

The school has nine elective and specialist teachers. If elective teachers positions were 20 percent of core teacher positions—the formula used in Chapter 2 to identify the number of elective teachers needed for a six-period schedule (admitting that elementary schools do not generally run on a schedule like middle and high schools do)—the 33 core teachers would trigger 6.6 positions for elective teachers, or 2.4 positions less than the nine in the school. The 9 positions suggest that elective classes are smaller than core classes on average, so a total of 2.4 positions could be freed up if elective class sizes were increased to that of core classes.

Note that as I assess the staffing in this school, my mind is simultaneously asking additional questions as it is looking for areas where cuts could not only be made to squeeze staffing into the budget constraint but also retain all the elements of Chapter 1's ambitious Plan of Action.

This school has eight categorical teachers; this total is a combination of teachers for struggling students from lower-income backgrounds (the school is 2/3 students from poverty backgrounds), students learning English (this school is 1/3 English language learners [ELL]), and students with mild and moderate disabilities including speech impairments (all staff for students with severe and profound disabilities have been excluded from this analysis). The table does not indicate how such teachers are deployed or used, however, though the Plan of Action has clear and specific strategies for them.

This school has a total of seven pupil support staff, including two guidance counselors and five others—probably some combination of nurses, social workers, psychologists, and perhaps some family liaison/case workers. In addition, there are two librarians in the school and three supervisory aides—paraprofessionals who help get students off the bus in the morning and on the bus in the afternoon, monitor recess and halls, and supervise the lunchroom.

Interestingly, this school, like many with significant numbers of students from lower-income backgrounds and thus recipients of a combination of federal Title I and state compensatory education dollars, has 20 instructional aides. As was clear in Chapter 2, instructional aides are endangered staff positions in this book, as randomized trial research—the gold standard of research—shows they do not add value to student achievement. Twenty instructional aides at $20,000 per aide equals $400,000, which possibly could be used more effectively.

In sum, I would argue this school is handsomely funded but has several examples of inefficient use of those dollars and the staffing resources bought with them.

Table 6.2 shows the funding required to support every element of the evidenced-based model of school improvement, discussed generally in Chapter 1 and in specific resource terms in Chapter 2. A quick overview of Table 6.2 shows two contrasts with Table 6.1. The first is that the cost of the Plan of Action is a bit less than the level of resources currently in the school, $5.24 million versus $5.32 million, so this school has sufficient resources to dramatically improve student performance. The second is that the allocation of staff to various roles in Table 6.2 is quite different from that in Table 6.1, so significant staff reallocation and school restructuring would be needed to execute Chapter 1's Plan of Action. But the overall level of resources exists to fully implement that powerful and effective improvement strategy.

Table 6.2 shows that the formulas in Chapter 2 would provide for only a part-time (0.39 or 0.40) assistant principal (as compared to the two in the current school) but provides for three full-time equivalent (FTE) positions of instructional facilitator or coach, compared to none in the current school. So the Plan of Action would actually increase the number of professionals on the instructional leadership team and admittedly change their roles.

The Plan of Action would actually increase the number of core teachers to almost 35, but reduce specialist/elective teachers to seven positions, for a total of 42 core and elective teachers. This compares to the 43 core and elective teachers in the current school.

The Plan of Action would provide for four full-time equivalent positions for teacher/tutors (which could be eight individuals tutoring for half their workload *and* doing something else—instructional coach, a core teacher, etc.—for the other half). The plan provides for 2 ESL teachers, 3.33 teachers for extended-day programming and another 3.33 positions for summer school programming, for a total of 12.66 positions for teachers to provide extra help for struggling students. To this number is added 4.2 teachers for providing services to students with moderate and mild disabilities plus an additional two aide positions. All totaled, the Plan of Action provides for nearly 17 professional teacher positions plus two aide positions to provide extra services to struggling students, as compared to the eight categorical program teachers in the current model.

But note that the Plan of Action has reallocated nearly all the instructional aide positions to certified teacher positions in the extra

Table 6.2   Highly Resourced Elementary School: Cost Feasibility of Chapter 1's Plan of Action

Elements of Model	Number of Positions	Cost of Positions
Principals	1	$110,000
Assistant principals	0.39	$33,056
Instructional facilitators	3	$210,000
Classroom teachers	34.67	$2,426,667
Elective and specialist teachers	6.93	$485,333
Teacher/tutors	4	$280,000
ESL/LEP teachers	2	$140,000
Extended-day teachers	3.33	$233,333
Summer School teachers	3.33	$233,333
Special Education teachers (non-severe)	4.17	$291,667
Special education aides (non-severe)	2.08	$47,917
Other pupil support	4	$280,000
Supervisory aides	2.78	$63,889
Librarians	1.39	$97,222
Secretary/clerk	2.78	$83,333
Discretionary Funds		
Professional development		$60,000
Equipment and technology		$150,000
Instructional materials		$84,000
Gifted and talented education		$15,000
Total Design Costs		**$5,243,740**

ELL = English language learners
ESL = English as a second language
LEP = limited English proficiency

help category, assuming (on the basis of research and best practices) both that professional teachers are more effective in providing such services and that most instructional aides as general teacher helpers do not add much value, as measured by the bottom line of improved student achievement. One could argue for retaining a few instructional aide positions instead of perhaps one teacher/tutor position to provide structured tutoring for students in the middle third of the achievement range but struggling with some reading problems. But as noted in Chapter 1, the Plan of Action does not call for many instructional aide positions.

Table 6.2 does include close to three supervisory aide positions as well as three secretary/clerk positions but drops the librarian positions from 2 to 1.4 (and many elementary schools might drop that to just 1.0 librarian and automate the book-lending operation of the library).

The two tables show that the current and proposed dollar resources for professional development training, technology, books and instructional materials, and gifted/talent education are about the same. So the staff use and budget challenge is more in the staffing areas.

So this school essentially starts from a position of being able to fully afford the ambitious Plan of Action that many districts and schools have used to dramatically boost student achievement, although the school has not used its resources in this way. So the first challenge for the school is to restructure its instructional program and to reallocate staff to this more effective Plan of Action.[1]

Now, how might this school cut its budget by 10 percent, or let's say $500,000? That is a pretty stiff challenge, but there are many possibilities. Let's eliminate the 0.39 assistant principal position for a savings of $33,000. Let's also eliminate the 0.39 librarian position for a savings of $27,000, which gives us a total savings now of $60,000.

Following the principle of being flexible about class size, recall that the Plan of Action calls for class sizes of 15 students in Grades K–3 and 25 students in Grades 4 and 5, which averages out to class sizes of 18 students across those six grades. Using the reallocation tool, raising class sizes to 20 in all Grades K–5 (still a pretty low number for most elementary schools across the country) would require about 4.5 fewer teacher positions and thus save nearly $400,000. Together with the modest assistant principal and librarian cuts, we have cut $460,000 and almost achieved our goal of a 10 percent cut of $500,000.

Few schools these days need to cut the budget 10 percent. For a well-funded elementary school, this exercise shows that a very modest increase in average class size—from 18 to 20—produces a budget cut just short of 10 percent. Modest flexibility about class size for this school certainly is the ticket to making a fairly large budget cut—with, I would argue, little if any negative impact on student learning.

This example points out that the major challenge for the school—even with a required budget cut of close to 10 percent—is not the budget cut but the restructuring of the school's instructional program to a more powerful set of programs embodied in Chapter 1's Plan of Action. I would expect that this would be the major challenge for many schools across the country, aside from fiscal pressures—to completely rethink their Plan of Action, especially if it has not been producing large improvements in student performance over the past several years. School restructuring (more than budget cuts) poses the stiffest challenge for this elementary school. And without a clear and powerful Plan of Action to guide resource priorities, budget cuts become even more onerous and potentially destructive.

An Underfunded High School

Table 6.3 shows what would be considered an under-resourced high school; this table and the subsequent table also are printouts from the school redesign and resource reallocation tool (available at http://cpre.wceruw.org/finance/redesign/schoolinfo.asp).

Excluding maintenance and operations, transportation, and food services, Table 6.3 shows that the total budget for this high school is just over $10 million—a big operation even though not so well funded. Indeed, 2,000-student high schools in all school districts are multimillion-dollar organizations! They need to be managed well in order for the millions of dollars spent to be transformed into effective instruction that produces high levels of student achievement. Let's assume that the task for this school is fund as much of the Plan of Action as is possible, knowing up front that its current resources are far from the level of those needed to do so.

The school has a principal and four assistant principals, which would be pretty typical for a 2,000-student high school; such schools often assign each assistant principal as the administrative director of each grade in the school—Grade 9, 10, 11, and 12. It has no instructional coaches.

This high school has a total of 120 professional teaching staff positions, including the librarians. Only about half (61) are core teachers. Dividing the total enrollment of 2,000 by 61 core teacher positions produces an average core class size of just under 33, about the core class size in many urban high schools across the county, including many that have produced large gains in student performance. This number is eight students larger than the class size in the Plan of Action.

This high school has 28 elective teachers, about 46 percent of core teachers, which is again not an atypical finding, as many high schools

Table 6.3 Slimly Resourced High School: Current Resources

Title	Positions (FTE)	Revenue Per Position	Total Revenues
Principal	1	$110,000	$110,000
Assistant principals	4	$85,000	$340,000
Instructional coach/support staff	0	$70,000	$0
Classroom teachers	61	$70,000	$4,270,000
Elective and specialist teachers	28	$70,000	$1,960,000
Categorical program teachers for mild special education, compensatory education, ESL, gifted and talented, etc.	20	$70,000	$1,400,000
Counselors	6	$70,000	$420,000
Other pupil support staff	3	$70,000	$210,000
Instructional aides	20	$23,000	$460,000
Supervisory aides	3	$20,000	$60,000
Librarians	2	$70,000	$140,000
Secretary/clerk	6	$30,000	$180,000
Discretionary Funds			
Professional development			$100,000
Equipment and technology			$300,000
Instructional materials			$300,000
Gifted and talented education			$20,000
Total of other discretionary funds			$0
Total Actual School Revenues			**$10,270,000**

ELL = English language learners
ESL = English as a second language
FTE = full-time equivalent

have numerous elective (noncore subject) classes. If the high school had a six-period schedule, it would require just 12.2 elective teachers (20 percent times 61), assuming elective classes were the same size as core classes. If the high school had a seven-period schedule, it would require just 24.4 elective teachers (40 percent times 61), assuming elective classes were the same size as core classes. So the school has more elective teachers than either a six- or seven-period schedule would require, meaning that the school might have even more than seven periods or that elective class sizes are smaller than core class sizes.

The school has 20 additional staff funded by categorical grants to provide services for students who are struggling because they are learning English (the school is 40 percent ELL), because they are from a lower-income background (the school if 50 percent poverty), or because they have a moderate or mild disability. In addition, the school has six guidance counselors with an average load of 333, a service load higher than the load included in the Plan of Action (which is one guidance counselor for every 250 students). The school also has two full-time librarian positions, not an excessive library staffing for a large high school.

In addition, the school has three supervisory aides and six secretaries and an acceptable amount of dollars for instructional materials and books, technology, and so on.

A quick look at Table 6.4 though shows that this high school is unable to fund the resources required for Chapter 1's Plan of Action. Its actual resources are $10.3 million while the Plan of Action requires $14.1 million, a difference of close to $4 million. Does this mean the school has no choices, that it simply cannot do much to improve student learning? The answer is absolutely not! Even though it cannot fully support the entire Plan of Action, it still has many important decisions to make about resource allocation and resource use. And it will need to make these decisions strategically, or it will end up not being able to boost its student performance.

The general objective for the budget dilemma faced by this school is to frame a budget that gives it a solid foundation for core instruction and at least some resources for extra help assistance for its struggling students, assuming that it won't be able to afford much else. Let's begin with the largest use of resources: core and elective teachers. And, following one of our major strategic budgeting principles, let's be flexible about class size. Table 6.4 shows that to have average core class sizes of 25 (much lower than the current class sizes of 33) and the same class sizes for elective classes but for a six-period day, the school would need 80 core teachers (substantially more than

Table 6.4   Slimly Resourced High School: Cost Feasibility of
Chapter 1's Plan of Action

Elements of Model	Number of Positions	Cost of Positions
Principals	1	$110,000
Assistant principals	2.33	$198,333
Instructional facilitators	10	$700,000
Classroom teachers	80	$5,600,000
Elective and specialist teachers	16	$1,120,000
Teacher/tutors	10	$700,000
ESL/LEP teachers	8	$560,000
Extended-day teachers	8.33	$583,333
Summer school teachers	8.33	$583,333
Special education teachers (non-severe)	13.33	$933,333
Special education aides (non-severe)	6.67	$153,333
Counselors	8	$560,000
Other pupil support	10	$700,000
Supervisory aides	10	$230,000
Librarians	3.33	$233,333
Secretary/clerk	13.33	$400,000

Discretionary Funds		
Professional development		$200,000
Equipment and technology		$500,000
Instructional materials		$350,000
Gifted and talented education		$50,000
Total Design Costs		**$14,112,145**

ELL = English language learners
ESL = English as a second language
FTE = full-time equivalent
LEP = limited English proficiency

it now has) and 16 elective teachers (substantially fewer than it now has), for a total core and elective teaching staff of 96 versus its current 89. But, if it increased average class size to 30, it would need only 80 teacher positions (66⅔ core and 13⅓ elective), fully 16 fewer positions. (Use the simulation tool to change the class size parameters and review staffing and cost changes to follow the staffing allocation in Table 6.5).

Note that this is somewhat more core and substantially fewer elective teachers than the school now has, but this is still in line with what the Plan of Action suggests for staffing effectively. Note also that with this number of core and elective teachers, the school can still provide a complete liberal arts curriculum, meet virtually all state high school graduation requirements, and maintain the full set of core and elective classes that would allow all students to take a full college preparatory set of courses sufficient in quality for admission to any university in the country, including elite universities.

Now, in order to maximize the effectiveness of core instruction, we need to organize teachers into collaborative teams so they can work together on curriculum and instructional issues. But that is difficult with a six-period schedule, as teachers provide instruction for five periods and have just one period a day for individual plan time. Chapter 3 suggested that the most straightforward way to provide collaborative time is to organize the school into a four-block schedule of 90 minutes each, having each teacher provide instruction for three blocks and then having pupil-free time for the remaining 90 minutes each day (a 30-minute lunch period is in addition to these instructional times). The concept is that this 90-minute period can be divided into two 45-minute periods—one for individual teacher plan time and one for collaborative team time. Or a school could have collaborative team time every other day for 90 minutes by alternating collaborative time and individual plan time. But to produce this organization, the school needs additional teachers—33 percent rather than just 25 percent above core teachers.

As Chapter 3 argued, however, when dollars area scarce, the most efficient way to provide these extra teachers so the school can organize teachers into collaborative teams would be to increase class size so that the block schedule requires the same number of core and elective teachers as the six-period schedule. For this school, that means increasing class sizes to 33, which is what the class sizes are today. The simulation shows that this would require just 80 teachers—60 core and 20 elective. But now there are 45 minutes a day (on average) not only for individual plan time but also for collaborative teacher work (or 90 minutes for each every other day).

Table 6.5 Strategic Allocation of High School Staffing Resources

Staffing Resource	Teaching Positions	Teaching Positions Left to Allocate	Instructional Aide Positions	Instructional Aide Positions Left to Allocate
Positions to start		120		20
Option 1: Core teacher class size of 30	$66^2/_3$			
Elective teachers for a six-period schedule	$13^1/_3$			
Total core and elective teachers	80	40	0	20
Option 2: Core teacher class size of 33	60			
Elective teachers for a four 90-minute block schedule	20			
Total core and elective teachers	80	40	0	20
Instructional Coaches: 4	84	36	0	20
Pupil support: 9	93	27		
Librarians: 2	95	25		
Special education: 13 teachers, 7 aides	108	12	7	13
ESL: 6 additional positions for a total of 8 positions, 2 taken from reallocating elective classes	6	6	0	13
Tutoring: total of 8 teachers, 2 created by reallocating 6 aide positions;				
7 trained instructional aide tutors	6	0	7	0

So now we have organized the school into four 90-minute blocks a day with 80 total teachers, class sizes of 33, and time for an average of 45 minutes of collaborative time and individual plan time a day (or 90 minutes for each every other day). And of the 120 total professional teaching positions in the school, we have used 80 for core and elective teachers, less than the 89 that exist in the school today. The major change has been a reduction in elective classes.

Chapters 1 and 3 argued, moreover, that in addition to collaborative time, teachers today also need the support of instructional coaches. The Plan of Action would provide 10 FTE instructional coach positions for this school (one for every 200 students). But that number obviously cannot be afforded. When faced with dollar constraints, many districts try to place at least one instructional coach into each school of 500 students, which would produce four instructional coach positions for this school. If that is done, we have used 84 of the possible 120 professional teaching positions.

For this exercise, we will leave counselors and pupil support staff as is, as well as the two librarians and the funds for professional development, technology, instructional materials, and gifted and talented educational programs. This allocates nine staff for pupil support and two for the librarians, bringing the number of professional staff positions used to 95 (84 plus 11). That means we have 25 professional staff positions left to allocate—as well as to decide how to use the 20 instructional aide positions.

The major remaining area is providing sufficiently for extra help programs, including the services students with mild and moderate disabilities need. The Plan of Action would provide 10 teacher/tutors, eight ESL teachers, $16\frac{2}{3}$ teachers for extended-day programs and summer school help, and $13\frac{1}{3}$ teacher and $6\frac{2}{3}$ aide positions for special education, for a total of $47\frac{1}{3}$ teacher and $6\frac{2}{3}$ aide positions—far beyond the positions remaining. This makes it tough to decide how to proceed. All decisions have downsides.

Legally, the school might have to first put a priority on special education; this would take 13 of the 25 professional staff positions and let's say 7 of the aide positions, leaving 12 professional and 13 aide positions remaining.

Providing ESL services for students learning English is also required, with almost the same legal authority as services for special education. Let's assume that when students are given ESL instruction, remaining elective classes can be combined for a savings of two teacher positions, meaning we need to take just six of the remaining professional positions to provide eight ESL positions (keep following the cumulating totals in Table 6.5).

Thus, there are six professional positions and 13 aide positions remaining, which I would suggest be focused on intensive extra help services for students still struggling, including some tutoring. I would suggest turning six of the aid positions into two more professional tutoring positions (as three aide positions equals the cost of one teacher position), thus providing eight professional tutoring or intervention positions and seven instructional aide positions. I would turn those aide positions into extra help tutoring in reading, writing, and mathematics, using a specific extra help program for students who are in the middle, but not the bottom, of the achievement levels but who are still struggling. These aides would be under the supervision of teachers providing intensive help in the same areas.

This budget allocation exercise follows the six macro-principles delineated above. It is not a fun exercise, because I would argue that this high school is underfunded. I also would argue that the proposed use of staff is a more effective use than is reflected in the current school, with its heavy reliance on a multiplicity of elective classes and many instructional aides providing general services for teachers. Though one could argue with the approach I have suggested, this approach reflects the Plan of Action, its core features, and its priorities—first to provide the best possible initial instruction by organizing teachers into collaborative groups assisted by instructional coaching, then to provide intensive extra help services (such as tutoring for struggling students) while also providing legally required services to ESL students and students with disabilities. Unfortunately, this school cannot afford any extended-day programs or summer school services, which I would argue would help it be even more effective; but the money is not there for those services.

This school could also provide double periods of reading and math for students struggling in these areas, with the levels of staff that have been suggested. The double period approach has been tried successfully by several middle and high schools around the country; it is essentially a no-extra-cost approach, as it substitutes some course (often an elective) for an extra period of reading or mathematics.

It would be very difficult for this high school to cut 5 percent from this slim budget. A 5 percent cut would require finding $500,000 to cut. Half perhaps could be taken from the instructional materials and technology dollars, though that would put those resources at risk of becoming outdated in future years. I leave it to the reader to find additional cuts, which certainly would be cuts into the remaining instructional meat of this school.

This discussion must end with one major point: *None* of the suggested cuts above represent fat in the system. All the cuts or all the resources that cannot be provided for in Table 6.4 are resources needed to fully fund the Plan of Action. One could only argue that the school could cut fat if it had more than the resources to fully fund the Plan of Action, but this example is $4 million short of that mark. So we are allocating the insufficient instructional meat it has, not trimming instructional fat.

A Modestly Funded Middle School

Table 6.6 shows what would be considered a modestly resourced middle school. Excluding maintenance and operations, transportation, and food services, the table shows that the total budget for this middle school is $3.96 million dollars, so it also is a multimillion-dollar operation. In comparing the bottom cost line in Table 6.7 with that in Table 6.6, this middle school is close but not able to fully afford the Plan of Action, so the budget exercise will first address how it could allocate resources to fund as much of the Plan of Action as possible.

The school has a principal and one assistant principal. The school also has no instructional coaches or facilitators. This leadership staffing is fairly typical for many middle schools.

It has 22 core subject classroom teachers—teachers who provide instruction in mathematics, reading/English/language arts/writing, science, history, and world language. Dividing the number of pupils (600) by 22 produces an average class size of just over 27—not super-large but above the Plan of Action's class size number of 25.

The school has 10 elective and specialist teachers. If elective teachers were 20 percent of core teachers—the formula used in Chapter 2 to identify the number of elective teachers needed for a six-period schedule—the 22 core teachers would trigger 4.4 positions for elective teachers, or 5.4 positions less than the 10 in the school. A seven-period middle school would require elective teachers at the rate of 40 percent of core teachers, or 8.8 positions—still less than the 10 in the school. The 10 elective teacher positions suggest that there are numerous elective courses in the school (typical of many if not most middle schools), that the school probably has a seven-period schedule (also typical of most middle schools today), and that elective classes are smaller than core classes on average (because there are more than needed, even for the seven-period day).

Pupil support staff is modest. Though the school has three counselors (probably one for each grade), it does not have any additional pupil support staff, which it should, given that 2/3 of its student come from lower-income backgrounds.

Table 6.6   Modestly Resourced Middle School: Current Resources

Title	Positions (FTE)	Revenue Per Position	Total Revenues
Principal	1	$110,000	$110,000
Assistant principals	1	$85,000	$85,000
Instructional support staff	0	$70,000	$0
Classroom teachers	22	$70,000	$1,540,000
Elective and specialist teachers	10	$70,000	$700,000
Categorical program teachers for mild special education, compensatory education, ESL, gifted and talented, etc.	10	$70,000	$700,000
Counselors	3	$70,000	$210,000
Other pupil support staff	0	$70,000	$0
Instructional aides	10	$23,000	$230,000
Supervisory aides	2	$20,000	$40,000
Librarians	1	$70,000	$70,000
Secretary/clerk	2	$30,000	$60,000
Discretionary Funds			
Professional development			$20,000
Equipment and technology			$100,000
Instructional materials			$84,000
Gifted and talented education			$10,000
Total of other discretionary funds			$0
Total Actual School Revenues			**$3,959,000**

ELL = English language learners
ESL = English as a second language
FTE = full-time equivalent

Table 6.7   Modestly Resourced Middle School: Cost Feasibility of Chapter 1's Plan of Action

Elements of Model	Number of Positions	Cost of Positions
Principals	1	$110,000
Assistant principals	0.33	$28,333
Instructional facilitators	3	$210,000
Classroom teachers	24	$1,680,000
Elective and specialist teachers	4.8	$336,000
Teacher/tutors	4	$280,000
ESL/LEP teachers	3	$210,000
Extended-day teachers	3.33	$233,333
Summer school teachers	3.33	$233,333
Special education teachers (non-severe)	4	$280,000
Special education aides (non-severe)	2	$46,000
Counselors	2.4	$168,000
Other pupil support	4	$280,000
Supervisory aides	2.67	$61,333
Librarians	1.33	$93,333
Secretary/clerk	2.67	$80,000
Discretionary Funds		
Professional development		$60,000
Equipment and technology		$150,000
Instructional materials		$84,000
Gifted and talented education		$15,000
Total Design Costs		**$4,563,810**

ELL = English language learners
ESL = English as a second language
LEP = limited English proficiency

This middle school has 10 categorically funded teaching staff and 10 instructional aides, most funded from state and federal programs for students from lower-income backgrounds, from families whose native language is not English, and for students with mild and moderate disabilities (recall that this budgeting exercise does not address funding and staff for students with severe disabilities—funds which are often quite large). We are not provided information about how these staff are used.

Finally, the school has two supervisory aides, one librarian, and two secretaries, which represent modest staffing in these areas. We should also note that the school has some money for training, about ⅔ of the funds it needs for computer technologies (at $250 a student), adequate funding for books and related instructional materials, and a small amount of money for gifted and talented educational services.

In comparing the actual budget for this school—$3.96 million—with the amount needed to fully fund the Plan of Action—$4.56 million—the budget exercise initially is to find an additional $600,000 or modify the Plan of Action's formulas by $600,000 (i.e., to a level where the key features of the plan could be funded). $600,000 equals about 8.5 teacher positions (remember also that it takes about three instructional aide positions to fund one teacher position).

One place to begin the strategic budgeting exercise for this school is class size.[2] As noted above, current class size is 27. But recall that the Plan of Action calls for class sizes of 25, so the data in Table 6.7 reflect a class size of 25. If the 25 number were increased to 27, the cost of the Plan of Action would drop from 28.8 to 26.7 teacher positions, or by about $150,000—a bit more than two teacher positions, meaning there is more fiscal squeezing that must be done. But our cost reduction target is now $450,000 ($600,000 minus $150,000).

Since I have worked with several schools in this kind of bind, it has become clear that there are no easy paths forward. But recall that the next objective is to find some collaborative teacher time, and that is best done initially by organizing the school on some sort of block schedule. And as done previously, we will simulate this approach with the same number of teachers—now 26.7—needed for the six-period day. Using the simulation tool, a class size of 30 with a block schedule—meaning elective teachers are produced at the rate of 33 percent of core teachers—also requires 26.6 teacher positions. And this approach provides teachers with both a 45-minute daily individual plan time and a 45-minute daily collaborative team time, or 90 minutes for each every other day.

At this point, having been flexible about class size, we have average class sizes of 30, considerable teacher collaborative team time, and three instructional coaches, which gives us the resources necessary to improve and make very effective the foundational instructional practices in all classrooms and all subjects. We still need to cut $450,000 from the school's budget, though.

The model also now provides for 4 teacher/tutor positions, 3 ESL teachers, 3.33 teacher positions for extended-day programming, another 3.33 teacher positions for summer school programming, 4 teachers and 2 aides for providing services to the students with mild and moderate disabilities, 6.4 positions for pupil support (which could cover the original 3 counselor positions plus 3.4 other positions), somewhat more supervisory aides, librarians, and secretarial support, and a total of $95,000 more than it now has for professional development, technology equipment, and gifted education. But we still need to drop our costs by $450,000.

Let's work backwards. Let's not increase the dollar-per-pupil figures. So let's drop $90,000 from those areas—leaving the additional for gifted and talented education. Let's also drop the ⅓ assistant principal position, as we have added three instructional coaches to the leadership team. That saves another $28,000. These cuts total $118,000, which when subtracted from $450,000 now leaves our funding gap at $332,000. Let's leave secretary, library, and supervisory aide figures as they were in the original middle school, reducing our budget gap now to $270,000.

At this point, I am trying to retain all the extra help services—teacher/tutors, ESL teachers, extended-day programs, summer school programs, and special education. So I next look critically at the pupil support staff. The allocations have increased from the original 3 counselors to 6.4 positions (including counselors). Let's say the school should retain the three counselors and add a family liaison and/or a nurse. That staffing approach would produce 4 pupil support positions, saving 2.4 positions, at an additional savings of $168,000 (2.4 times $70,000). The budget shortfall is now just $104,000 ($270,000 minus $168,000), which is about 1.5 professional positions.

Given the relatively weak findings on extended-day programs (*relatively* weak but not *absolutely* so) and our knowledge that summer learning loss does occur and in greater amounts for students from lower-income backgrounds, I'd probably take the remaining 1.5 professional positions that must be cut from the 3.33 positions for the extended-day programming.

Doing that brings my school into budget balance. I have produced a feasible budget and have retained the bulk of the services and strategies in the Plan of Action, though significant school restructuring would be needed to implement the Plan of Action, as its use of staff and dollar resources is quite different from current practice.

Finally, if the budget had to be further cut by, say 5 to 7 percent, I'd probably keep everything and cut the extended-day and summer school programming. I would not be happy doing so, but that is where I would make the next set of cuts.

Again, none of these cuts are cutting fat in the system; they are cutting or not resourcing instructional meat that a full Plan of Action would require. But even though short of full funding, I would argue the Plan of Action represents a more effective use of the resources that exist.

Value Judgments as Part of Strategic Budgeting

Clearly, I have made value judgments in these budget-cutting exercises. A big one is being flexible about class size, which has risen from 27 to 30 and even 33 in the high school. Another value judgment is the strong focus on making core instructional practice as strong and effective as possible by providing ample collaborative teacher time (with no late-start days or early release of students) and retaining the full coterie of instructional coaches in all but the high school, which still has some instructional coaches. Professional development has been critical to all the schools and districts that dramatically increased student achievement, and the professional development includes work by collaborative teacher teams with support provided by instructional coaches.

Another value judgment—again driven by research and best practices on what works to boost academic learning—has been to retain almost all or many of the extra help strategies: teacher/tutors, ESL teachers, some extended-day programming, summer school, and special education. These services are particularly important for schools with significant numbers of students from poverty and ELL backgrounds; a comprehensive set of ongoing extra help programs will be needed to get students in such schools up to and over rigorous proficiency performance bars.

But these value judgments I believe are professionally based, as they support the programs and strategies dozens and dozens of schools across America have deployed in their processes of boosting student learning—and reducing achievement gaps—by large increments.

On the other hand, others might have different professional judgments that would guide budget decisions. I would say fine—as long as they produce schools that boost student learning, which also would be the test for future budget decisions and program strategies suggested above.

Note also that in these strategic budget exercises, I have resisted the cost pressures on schools. Assuming the budget is tight—at the minimum not going up—I have a situation of salary freezes (so automatic salary hikes don't allow my budget year to begin in a fiscal hole). And I have not reduced class sizes or expanded electives; in fact, I have increased class sizes and reduced (but not eliminated) electives. I have focused on what it takes to boost student academic learning in core subjects. And as stated earlier, school and district leaders will need broader political support to move these decisions forward, because they are at odds with public cost pressures.

Additional Budget-Cutting Efforts

The above budget exercises have all focused on the staff and dollars in the instruction, instructional support, pupil support, and school administrative parts of school expenditures, because as they say, that is where most of the money is. If big efficiencies are to be found, one has to begin in the big budget areas.

Nevertheless, if schools and districts have not already done so, they clearly should review all areas:

- Districts have been conducting energy audits and finding many ways to save in those areas; often, management-consulting companies will offer to find places to save money and take any consulting fee only when cost reductions emerge.
- Transportation costs often can be trimmed, perhaps by outsourcing in many places.
- Outsourcing food services also often reduces food costs.
- Trimming central offices sometimes still might be possible in some districts; for example, that is what the new superintendent did in Chicago before the 2011–2012 school year began. Certainly, large districts should conduct central office/professional development fiscal and program audits as discussed in Chapter 3 to potentially free up significant resources to support an ongoing comprehensive professional development system.

The point of these comments is to say that there might be other portions of the overall school or district budget where efficiencies can be found. This book has shown that the major inefficiencies have been in the instruction, instructional support, pupil support, and school administrative portions of the budget. And the book has argued that the first step in strategic budgeting is to align current staffing and dollar resources in these areas of school budgets to the resource needs of a comprehensive and proven-effective Plan of Action, which is described in Chapters 1 and 2. That clearly is the first step.

Tap Technology

Finally, this book argues that all schools should seriously consider tapping the power of computer technology. Generally, I have left the technology dollars in all school examples. If so equipped, schools can offer any semester course for $500 per pupil, which is our Chapter 5 upward-bound estimate for such offerings. Indeed, the entire school program of 12 semester courses can be offered for just $6,000 per pupil. All Advanced Placement (AP) classes can be offered at these cost levels—so in these tight budget times, AP courses should *not* be cut. If money is tight, offer AP courses in an online format—not as an extra cost. Offer them with no on-site teacher but only the teacher support provided by the AP course online provider.

Last, schools should review the possibilities of moving to blended-instruction approaches, which allow for more students per teacher supplemented with an extensive set of online course and instructional program offerings. Again, this is a real option; many schools are moving toward this area, and such approaches can be effective even in schools with large concentrations of students from lower-income backgrounds and non-English-speaking students, such as the Rocketship Mateo Sheedy Elementary School in San Jose, California.

Summary

How scarce education resources are used to resource effective curriculum and instructional strategies is very important. In these times of shrinking resources, cutting budgets without thinking strategically about which programs should be cut and which should be retained will only result in lower levels of student performance. This entire book has addressed numerous issues related to how scarce resources can be used in the most effective manner. Business as usual, budget cutting as usual, won't work in today's environment—the stakes are too high. All education leaders, including teachers, need to think strategically about education budgets so that progress on improving student performance can continue even when the budgets get tight.

Strategic budgeting is the process of closely aligning resource use to strategies and programs that are known to work, all of which are embodied in a Plan of Action. This book has identified one powerful Plan of Action, the resource needs of each element of that Plan of Action, and recommended budget steps for schools in various budget contexts to resource that Plan of Action, including schools with declining fiscal resources.

As the examples show, strategic budgeting entails setting priorities even for the various elements in the Plan of Action, understanding what the foundational elements of the Plan are and when cuts must be made, making those cuts in ways that retain the critical elements of the Plan of Action.

The book argues that the foundational core of the Plan of Action is Tier 1 or core instruction in every subject and the elements that make that instruction as effective as possible. That includes first recruiting and retaining effective teachers in every classroom. It includes having high and rigorous goals for improved student learning in all classes and embedding every teacher in a context that continually helps them improve their instructional expertise. Thus, the book sets a priority on having time carved out of school schedules for teachers to engage in collaborative work on the instructional program, using short cycle interim assessments of student performance to continuously hone their instructional strategies, and doing all this with the assistance of instructional coaches.

The book thus makes recruiting high-quality teachers a top priority, investing in intensive and ongoing professional development a top priority, and time for both individual planning work and collaborative work a top priority. The book gives higher priority to these programmatic elements than to smaller class sizes, allowing class sizes to grow into the low 30s in some rare cases.

This book also firmly believes that nearly all students can achieve high standards. Thus, in addition to resourcing the elements that make core instruction as effective as possible, the book recommends a series of interventions for struggling students that keep the performance standards high and expand learning time—first through one-to-one (and up to one-to-five) tutoring during the regular school day and then through some combination of extended-day and summer school programming. When resources are scarce, the book sets a priority on providing at least some small-group tutoring for struggling students. Such intensive intervention has huge payoffs for students.

All of the recommendations in this book, even those for schools with very limited resources, allow all schools to provide a range of elective classes and a full liberal arts curriculum. But this book warns districts and schools to resist the pressures from across America to continuously add more electives, arguing that excessive electives courses not only have little (if any) positive impact on student learning in core subjects but consume large amounts of resources, both of which limit the degree to which schools can deploy their resources strategically.

The book has been clear that unless funds are generous, schools must resist the cost pressures to lower class size and increase electives, as these strategies eat up large chunks of the budget and (except for small classes in the first four grades) have no research that they positively impact student achievement.

The book also recommends that educators rethink how teacher and principal talent is recruited, placed, developed, evaluated, and paid. It outlines ways urban districts can partner with national teacher and principal talent recruitment organizations to recruit higher-caliber teachers and principals than the district can do on its own—and often at a lower cost. The book reinforces the national movement to develop rigorous indicators of teacher and principal effectiveness and to use them in key human resource management decisions, particularly linked to tenure, promotion, retention, and dismissal. The book also recommends redesigning educator salary schedules to trigger major pay increases on the basis of the effectiveness measures, thus moving away from experience as the prime factor that boosts educator salaries. And the book recommends education systems shift, over time, to portable cash balance retirement programs; these programs align pension payouts to individual and system contributions and accrued investment gains thus making them economically fair, cater to the mobile workers of today, and allow individuals to retire anytime they want, with their retirement annuity linked to the cash balance value of their portfolio rather than to various elements that today artificially spike teacher retirements at different ages.

Further, the book strongly argues that the time has come for schools to accede to the power of technology and the many online learning opportunities that exist today. From state-supported virtual schools to virtual charter schools to private-sector-based online programs, nearly all educational courses can be taken from kindergarten to Grade 12 (including nearly all Advanced Placement courses) in online formats, all of which are much more cost-effective than traditional brick-and-mortar schooling. As just one final example, students can take a full load of courses through the Florida Virtual School at about $6,000 to $7,000 a year, much less than is spent in any district school. When budgets are tight, educators would be foolish to ignore the upside potential of online learning.

Finally, a recently developed district budget tool called Budget Hold 'Em has just been developed (http://holdem.erstools.org/card-game/index.html). It provides districts a series of budget alternatives—some cuts and some enhancements—together with budget constraints and guidance as to which options have research support to invoke. Districts might start with this overall budget tool before getting into the specifics of resource allocation at each school, as has been the focus in this chapter.

Notes

1. Note that this book uses the Plan of Action in Chapter 1 as the vision for how to organize schools and use resources. It could be that other Plans of Action could drive school organization and staff use, but the Plan in Chapter 1 has been consistently used by dozens and dozens of schools across America. At a generic level, the discussion for the three schools in this chapter shows how a specific Plan of Action can be used to rethink the use of staffing resources. If a different and as-effective Plan of Action were known, schools could use that instead. The point is to assess staffing levels and staff use via some Plan of Action that is known to work (i.e., to lead to large gains in student learning and achievement).

2. Actually, class size is probably the starting point for nearly every school, as class size for core and elective teachers consumes the vast bulk of school budgets, so it is best to start where the money is.

References

Anderson, A. H., Augenblick, J., DeCesare, D., & Conrad, J. (2006). *Costs and funding of virtual schools.* Denver, CO: Augenblick, Palaich, and Associates. Also retrieved from http://www.inacol.org/research/docs/Costs&Funding.pdf

Aportela, A., & Goetz, M. (2008a). *Strategic management of human capital: New leaders for new schools.* Madison: University of Wisconsin, Wisconsin Center for Education Research, Consortium for Policy Research in Education.

Aportela, A., & Goetz, M. (2008b). *Strategic management of human capital: The new teacher project.* Madison: University of Wisconsin, Wisconsin Center for Education Research, Consortium for Policy Research in Education.

Archer, J. (2000). The link to higher scores. In R. D. Pea (Ed.), *The Jossey-Bass reader on technology and learning* (pp. 112–123). San Francisco, CA: Jossey-Bass.

Archibald, S. (2008). *Strategic management of human capital: Boston.* Madison: University of Wisconsin, Wisconsin Center for Education Research, Consortium for Policy Research in Education.

Baum, M. (2011). *Using short-cycle interim assessment to improve educator evaluation, educator effectiveness, and student achievement.* Wisconsin Rapids, WI: Renaissance Learning.

Blankstein, A. M. (2010). *Failure is not an option: 6 principles for making student success the only option.* Thousand Oaks, CA: Corwin.

Bloom, B. (1984). The 2 sigma problem: The search for methods of group instruction as effective as one-to-one tutoring. *Educational Researcher, 13*(6), 4–16.

Borman, G., & Boulay, M. (Eds.). (2004). *Summer learning: Research, policies, and programs.* Mahwah, NJ: Lawrence Erlbaum Associates.

Borman, G., & Dowling, M. N. (2006). The longitudinal achievement effects of multi-year summer school: Evidence from the teach Baltimore randomized field trial. *Educational Evaluation and Policy Analysis, 28,* 25–48.

Borman, G., Slavin, R. E., Cheung, A., Chamberlain, A., Madden, N., & Chambers, B. (2007). Final reading outcomes of the national randomized field trial of success for all. *American Educational Research Journal, 44*(3), 701–731.

Boudett, K. P., City, E. A., & Murnane, R. (2007). *A step-by-step guide to using assessment results to improve teaching and learning.* Cambridge, MA: Harvard Education Press.

Boudett, K. P., & Steele, J. L. (2007). *Data wise in action: Stories of schools using data to improve teaching and learning.* Cambridge, MA: Harvard Education Press.

Boyd, D., Lankford, H., Loeb, S., Rockoff, J., & Wyckoff, J. (2008). *The narrowing gap in New York city teacher qualifications and its implications for student achievement in high-poverty schools.* Washington, DC: The Urban Institute, Center for Analysis of Longitudinal Data in Education Research.

Carlson, D., Borman, G. D., & Robinson, M. (2011). A multistate district-level cluster randomized trial of the impact of data-driven reform on reading and mathematics achievement. *Educational Evaluation and Policy Analysis, 33*(3), 378–398.

Cavanaugh, C. (2009). *Getting students more learning time online.* Washington, DC: Center for American Progress.

Center on Education Policy. (2011). *Districts foresee budget cuts, teacher layoffs and a slowing of education reform efforts.* Washington, DC: Author.

Chenoweth, K. (2007). *It's being done: Academic success in unexpected schools.* Cambridge, MA: Harvard Education Press.

Childress, S. M., Doyle, D. P., & Thomas, D. A. (2009). *Leading for equity: The pursuit of excellence in the Montgomery County public schools.* Cambridge, MA: Harvard Education Press.

Clark, R. E. (2010). Retiree health plans for public school teachers after GASB 43 and 45. *Education Finance and Policy, 4*(5), 438–462.

Clark, R. E., & Estes, F. (1999) The development of authentic educational technologies, *Educational Technology, 37*(2) 5–16.

Cooper, H., Charlton, K., Valentine, J. C., & Muhlenbruck, L. (2000). Making the most of summer school: A meta-analytic and narrative review. *Monographs of the Society for Research in Child Development, 65* (1, Serial No. 260).

Costrell, R. M., & Podgursky, M. (2009). Peaks, cliffs, and valleys: The peculiar incentives in teacher retirement systems and their consequences for school staffing. *Education Finance and Policy, 4*(2), 175–211.

Costrell, R. M., & Podgursky, M. (2010). Distribution of benefits in teacher retirement systems and their implications for mobility. *Education Finance and Policy, 4*(5), 519–557.

Crow, T. (Ed.). (2011). Standards for professional learning [Special issue]. *Journal of Staff Development, 32*(4).

Davis, M. R. (2011). Hybrid charters. *Digital directions,* Spring/Summer 2011, 28–31.

DeArmond, M., & Goldhaber, D. (2010). Scrambling the nest egg: How well do teachers understand their pensions, and what do they think about alternative pension structures? *Education Finance and Policy, 4*(5), 558–586.

Dillon, S. (2011, July 6). As budgets are trimmed, time in class is shortened. *New York Times,* p. A14.

Dobbie, W. (2011, July). *Teacher characteristics and student achievement: Evidence from teach for America.* Retrieved from http://www.people.fas.harvard.edu/~dobbie/research/TeacherCharacteristics_July2011.pdf

DuFour, R., DuFour, R., & Eaker, R. (2008). *Revisiting professional learning communities at work: New insights for improving schools.* Bloomington, IN: Solution Tree.

DuFour, R., DuFour, R., Eaker, R., & Karhanek, G. (2010). *Raising the bar and closing the gap: Whatever it takes.* Bloomington, IN: Solution Tree.

Earle, R. S. (2002). The integration of instructional technology into public education. *Educational Technology Magazine, 42*(1), 5–13. Retrieved August, 2010 from http://bookstoread.com/etp/earle.pdf

Education Trust. (2009). The education trust [website]. Retrieved from http://www.edtrust.org

Education Week. (2011). E-Learning for special populations [Supplement issue for August 24, 2011]. *Education Week, 31*(1), S1–S20.

Educational Leadership. (2007/2008). [Entire issue: Informative assessment]. *65*(4).

Elmore, R., & Burney, D. (1999). Investing in teacher learning: Staff development and instructional improvement. In L. Darling-Hammond & G. Sykes (Eds.), *Teaching as the learning profession: Handbook of policy and practice* (pp. 263–291). San Francisco, CA: Jossey-Bass.

Farr, S. (2010). *Teaching as leadership: The highly effective teacher's guide to closing the achievement gap.* San Francisco, CA: Jossey-Bass.

Fashola, O. S. (1998). *Review of extended-day and after-school programs and their effectiveness.* Baltimore, MD: Center for Research on the Education of Students Placed At Risk, Johns Hopkins University.

Felton, R. (2010). *An overview of reading: Reading problems and effective reading programs.* Los Angeles, CA: Lawrence O. Picus & Associates.

Finn, J. D., & Achilles, C. M. (1999). Tennessee's class size study: Findings, implications, misconceptions. *Educational Evaluation and Policy Analysis, 21,* 97–109.

Finn, J. D., Gerger, S. B., Achilles, C. M., & Zaharias, J. B. (2001). The enduring effects of small classes. *Teachers College Record, 103*(2), 145–183.

Friedberg, L., & Turner, S. (2010). Labor market effects of pensions and implications for teachers. *Education Finance and Policy, 4*(5), 463–491.

Fullan, M. (2010). *All systems go: The change imperative for whole system reform.* Thousand Oaks, CA: Corwin.

Fusaro, J. A. (1997). The effect of full day kindergarten on student achievement: A meta-analysis. *Child Study Journal, 27*(4), 269–277.

Goetz, M., & Aportela, A. (2008). *Strategic management of human capital: Teach for America.* Madison: University of Wisconsin, Wisconsin Center for Education Research, Consortium for Policy Research in Education.

Goertz, M., & Levin, S. (2008). *Strategic management of human capital: New York City.* Madison: University of Wisconsin, Wisconsin Center for Education Research, Consortium for Policy Research in Education.

Goldhaber, D., & Theobold, R. (2011). *Managing the teacher workforce in austere times: The implications of teacher layoffs.* Seattle: University of Washington, Center for Education Data & Research.

Hansen, J. (2010). An introduction to teacher retirement benefits. *Education Finance and Policy, 4*(5), 402–437.

Harris, D. N., & Adams, S. J. (2007). Understanding the level and causes of teacher turnover: A comparison with other professions. *Economics of Education Review, 26,* 325–337.

Heitin, L. (2011). Reliance grows for alternative certification. *Education Week, 30*(5), p. 5.

Henry, G., Thompson, C., Bastian, K. C., Fortner, C. K., Kershaw, D. C., Purtell, K. M., & Zulli, R. A. (2010). *Portal report: Teacher preparation and student test scores in North Carolina.* Chapel Hill: University of North Carolina, Carolina Institute for Public Policy.

Horn, M. B., & Staker, H. (2011). *The rise of K–12 blended learning.* Watertown, MA: Innosight Institute.

Howell, W. G., West, M. R., & Peterson, P. E. (2011). Public and Teachers Increasingly Divided on Key Education Issues. Retrieved from http://educationnext.org/public-and-teachers-increasingly-divided-on-key-education-issues

International Association for K–12 Online Learning (iNACOL). (2010). *A national primer on K–12 online learning, version 2.* Retrieved from http://www.inacol.org/research/docs/iNCL_NationalPrimerv22010-web.pdf

Kimball, S. (2008). *Strategic management of human capital: Chicago.* Madison: University of Wisconsin, Wisconsin Center for Education Research, Consortium for Policy Research in Education.

Konstantopoulos, S., & Chung, V. (2009). What are the long-term effects of small classes on the achievement gap? Evidence from the lasting benefits study. *American Journal of Education, 116*(1), 125–154.

Koppich, J. (2008). *Strategic management of human capital: Long Beach.* Madison: University of Wisconsin, Wisconsin Center for Education Research, Consortium for Policy Research in Education.

Krueger, A. (2002). Understanding the magnitude and effect of class size on student achievement. In L. Mishel & R. Rothstein (Eds.), *The class size debate* (pp. 7–35). Washington, DC: Economic Policy Institute.

Krueger, A., & Whitmore, D. M. (2001). *Would smaller classes help close the black-white achievement gap?* (Working paper #451). Princeton, NJ: Princeton University. Retrieved from http://www.irs.princeton.edu/pubs/pdfs/451.pdf.

Kulik, J. (1994). Meta-analytical studies of findings on computer-based instruction. In E. Baker & H. F. O'Neil, Jr. (Eds.), *Technology assessment in education and training* (pp. 9–34). Hillsdale, NJ: Erlbaum Associates.

Kulik, J. (2003). *Effects of using instructional technology in elementary and secondary schools: What controlled evaluation studies say* (SRI Project Number P10446.001). Arlington, VA: SRI International.

Lankford, H., Loeb, S., & Wyckoff, J. (2002). Teaching sorting and the plight of urban schools. *Educational Evaluation and Policy Analysis, 24*(61), 37–62.

Lee, V., & Smith, J. (1997). High school size: Which works best, and for whom? *Educational Evaluation and Policy Analysis, 19*(3), 205–228.

Levenson, N. (2011). *Something has got to change: Rethinking special education* (Working Paper #2011–01). Washington, DC: American Enterprise Institute.

Levin, J. D., & Quinn, M. (2003). *Missed opportunities: How we keep high-quality teachers out of urban classrooms.* New York, NY: The New Teacher Project. Retrieved from http://www.newteacherproject.org/report.html

Louis, K. S., & Marks, H. M. (1998). Does professional community affect the classroom? Teachers' work and student experiences in restructuring schools. *American Journal of Education, 106*(4), 532–575.

Madden, N. A., Slavin, R., Karweit, N., Dolan, L. J., & Wasik, B. A. (1993). Success for all: Longitudinal effects of a restructuring program for inner-city elementary schools. *American Educational Research Journal, 30,* 123–148.

Marks, H.M., & Louis, K.S. (1997). Does teacher empowerment affect the classroom? The implications of teacher empowerment for teachers' instructional practice and student academic performance. *Educational Evaluation and Policy Analysis, 19*(3) 245–275.

Mass Insight Education. (2011). Mass insight education [website]. Retrieved from http://www.massinsight.org

McCombs, J. S., Augustine, C. H., Schwartz, H. L., Bodilly, S. J., McInnis, B., Lichter, D. S., & Cross, A. B. (2011). *Making summer count: How summer programs can boost children's learning.* Santa Monica, CA: The RAND Corporation.

Means, B., Toyama, Y., Murphy, R., Bakia, M., & Jones, K. (2009). *Evaluation of evidence-based practices in online learning: A meta-analysis and review of online learning studies.* Washington, DC: United States Department of Education.

Milanowski, A. (2008a). *Do teacher pay levels matter?* Madison: University of Wisconsin, Wisconsin Center for Education Research, Consortium for Policy Research in Education.

Milanowski, A. (2008b). *How to pay teachers for student performance outcomes.* Madison: University of Wisconsin, Wisconsin Center for Education Research, Consortium for Policy Research in Education.

Milanowski, A. (2011). Strategic measures of teacher performance. *Phi Delta Kappan, 92*(7), 19–25.

Milanowski, A., Heneman, H. G., III, & Kimball, S. (2009). *Review of teaching performance assessments for use in human capital management.* Madison: University of Wisconsin, Wisconsin Center for Education Research, Consortium for Policy Research in Education. Retrieved from http://www.smhc-cpre.org/resources/

Milanowski, A., & Odden, A. (2007). *A new approach to the cost of teacher turnover* (Working Paper #13). Seattle: University of Washington, Evans School of Public Policy, Center on Reinventing Public Education, School Finance Redesign Project.

Miles, K. H., & Frank, S. (2008). *The strategic school: Making the most of people, time, and money.* Thousand Oaks, CA: Corwin.

Miles, K. H., Odden, A., Fermanich, M., & Archibald, S. (2004). Inside the black box of school district spending on professional development: Lessons from five urban districts. *Journal of Education Finance, 30*(1), 1–26.

Monahan, A. B. (2010). Public pension plan reform: The legal framework. *Education Finance and Policy, 4*(5), 617–636.

Newmann, F., and Associates. (1996). *Authentic achievement: Restructuring schools for intellectual quality.* San Francisco, CA: Jossey-Bass.

Noell, G. H., & Gansl, K. A. (2009). *Teach for America teachers' contribution to student achievement in Louisiana in grades 4–9: 2004–2005 to 2006–2007.* Baton Rouge: Louisiana Department of Education, Division of Planning, analysis and Information Resources. Retrieved from www.nctq.org/docs/TFA_Louisiana_study.PDF

Nye, B., Hedges, L. V., & Konstantopulos, S. (2001). The long-term effects of small classes in early grades: Lasting benefits in mathematics achievement at grade nine. *Journal of Experimental Education, 69*(3), 245–258.

Nye, B., Hedges, L. V., & Konstantopoulos, S. (2002). Do low-achieving students benefit more from small classes? Evidence from the Tennessee class size experiment. *Educational Evaluation & Policy Analysis, 24*(3), 201–217.

Odden, A. (2008a). *How to fund teacher compensation changes.* Madison: University of Wisconsin, Wisconsin Center for Education Research, Consortium for Policy Research in Education.

Odden, A. (2008b). *New teacher pay structures: The compensation side of the strategic management of human capital.* Madison: University of Wisconsin, Wisconsin Center for Education Research, Consortium for Policy Research in Education.

Odden, A. (2009). *Ten strategies for doubling student performance.* Thousand Oaks, CA: Corwin.

Odden, A. (2011a). *Strategic management of human capital in education.* New York, NY: Routledge.

Odden, A. (2011b). The dollars and sense of comprehensive professional learning. *Journal of Staff Development, 32*(4), 26–32.

Odden, A., & Archibald, S. (2001). *Reallocating resources: How to boost student achievement without spending more.* Thousand Oaks, CA: Corwin.

Odden, A., & Archibald, S. (2009). *Doubling student performance . . . and finding the resources to do it.* Thousand Oaks, CA: Corwin.

Odden, A., Borman, G., & Fermanich, M. (2004). Assessing teacher, classroom, and school effects, including fiscal effects. *Peabody Journal of Education, 79*(4), 4–32.

Odden, A., Goetz, M., & Picus, L. O. (2008). Using available evidence to estimate the cost of educational adequacy. *Education Finance and Policy, 3*(3), 374–397.

Odden, A., Goetz, M., & Picus, L. O. (2010). Merging costs with effective resource strategies. In J. Adams, Jr. (Ed.), *Smart money: Using educational resources to accomplish ambitious learning goals* (pp. 141–156). Cambridge, MA: Harvard Education Press.

Odden, A., & Picus, L. O. (2008). *School finance: A policy perspective* (4th ed.). New York, NY: McGraw-Hill.

Odden, A., & Picus, L. O. (2010). *Career technical education.* (Report prepared for the Wyoming Select Committee on Recalibration). Cheyenne, WY: Legislative Services Organization.

Odden, A., & Picus, L. O. (2011). Improving teaching and learning when budgets are tight. *Phi Delta Kappan, 93*(1), 42–48.

Odden, A., Picus, L. O., & Goetz, M. (2010). A 50 state strategy to achieve school finance adequacy. *Educational Policy, 24*(4), 628–654.

Ohio Legislative Committee on Education Oversight. (2005). *The Operating Costs of Ohio's eCommunity Schools.* Columbus, OH: Legislative Office of Education Oversight.

O'Toole, J., & Lawler, E. E., III. (2006). *The new American workplace.* New York, NY: Palgrave Macmillan.

Partin, E. (2010). *Did you know? Fiscal impact of raising student-teacher ratios in Ohio.* Dayton, OH: Fordham Institute. Retrieved July 2011 from http://www.educationgadfly.net/flypaper/2010/07/did-you-know-fiscal-impact-of-raising-student-teacher-ratios-in-ohio/

Patall, E., Cooper, H., & Allen, A. B. (2011). Extending the school day or year: A systematic review of research (1985–2009). *Review of Educational Research, 80*(3), 401–436.

Pew Research Center. (2010). *Millennials: A portrait of generation Next: Confident. Connected. Open to change.* Retrieved from http://pewsocialtrends.org/assets/pdf/millennials-confident-connected-open-to-change.pdf

Phelps, L. A. (2006). *Career and technical education in Wisconsin's new economy: Challenges and investment imperatives.* (Paper prepared for the Wisconsin School Finance Adequacy Task Force). Madison: University of Wisconsin, Wisconsin Center for Education Research.

Pianta, R., Allen, J., & King, H. (2011). An interaction-based approach to enhancing secondary school instruction and student achievement. *Science, 333*(6045), 1034–1037.

Picus, L. O., Odden, A., Aportela, A., Mangan, M. T., & Goetz, M. (2008). *Implementing school finance adequacy: School level resource use in Wyoming following adequacy-oriented finance reform.* (Report prepared for the Wyoming Legislative Service Office). North Hollywood, CA: Lawrence O. Picus and Associates. Retrieved from http://legisweb.state.wy.us/2008/interim/schoolfinance/Resources.pdf

Prensky, M. (2010). *Teaching digital natives: Partnering for real learning.* Thousand Oaks, CA: Corwin.

Price, S., Odden, A., & Picus, L. O. (2010). *Recalibration of instructional materials and technology costs.* (Report prepared for the Wyoming Select Committee on Recalibration). Cheyenne, WY: Legislative Services Organization.

Raudenbusch, S. (2009). The *Brown* legacy and the O'Connor challenge: Transforming schools in the images of children's potential. *Educational Researcher, 38*(3), 169–180.

Roblyer, M. D. (2005). Educational Technology Research That Makes a Difference: Series Introduction. *Contemporary Issues in Technology and Teacher Education* [Online serial], *5*(2). Retrieved from http://www.cite-journal.org/vol5/iss2/seminal/article1.cfm

Roza, M. (2010). *Educational economics: Where do school funds go?* Washington, DC: Urban Institute Press.

Schrum, L. M., & Levine, B. B. (2009). *Leading 21st century schools: Harnessing technology for engagement and achievement.* Thousand Oaks, CA: Corwin.

Slavin, R. (1996). Neverstreaming: Preventing learning disabilities. *Educational Leadership, 53*(5), 4–7.

Slavin, R. E., Madden, N., Calderon, M., Chamberlain, A., & Hennessy, M. (2011). Reading and language outcomes of a multi-year randomized evaluation of transitional bilingual education. *Educational Evaluation & Policy Analysis, 33*(3), 47–58.

Spillane, J. (2006). *Distributed leadership.* San Francisco, CA: Jossey-Bass.

Staker, H. (2011). *The rise of K–12 blended learning: Profiles of emerging models.* Retrieved in July 2011 from http://www.innosightinstitute.org/innosight/wp-content/uploads/2011/05/The-Rise-of-K-12-Blended-Learning.pdf

Stringfield, S., Ross, S. M., & Smith, L., (1996). *Bold plans for school restructuring: The New American Schools designs.* Mahwah, NJ: Lawrence Erlbaum.

Teach For America. (2010). *Retention report.* New York, NY: Teach For America.

Tennessee Higher Education Commission. (2010). *2010 report card on the effectiveness of teacher training programs.* Nashville, TN: Tennessee Higher Education Commission.

Texas Center for Education Research. (2000). *The cost of teacher turnover.* (Paper prepared for the Texas State Board for Educator Certification). Austin, TX: Author.

Thayer, J. (2004). *Professional development: Costs and effectiveness in one rural district.* (Unpublished doctoral dissertation). University of Wisconsin–Madison.

Torgeson, J. K. (2004). Avoiding the devastating downward spiral. *American Educator, 28*(3), 6–19, 45–47.

U.S. Department of Education. (2010a). *Educational technology in public school districts: Fall 2008.* Washington DC: National Center for Education Statistics. Retrieved from http://nces.ed.gov/pubs2010/2010003.pdf

U.S. Department of Education. (2010b). *Transforming American education: Learning powered by technology.* Retrieved from http://www.ed.gov/sites/default/files/NETP-2010-final-report.pdf

Watson, J., Murin, A., Vashaw, L., Gemin, B., & Rapp, C. (2010). *Keeping pace with K–12 online learning: An annual review of policy and practice.* Durango, CO: Evergreen Education Group. Retrieved from http://www.kpk12.com/cms/wp-content/uploads/KeepingPaceK12_2010.pdf

Weisberg, D., Sexton, S., Mulhern, J., & Keeling, D. (2009). *The widget effect: Our national failure to acknowledge and act on differences in teacher effectiveness.* New York, NY: The New Teacher Project. Retrieved from http://widgeteffect.org/downloads/TheWidgetEffect.pdf

Wise, B., & Rothman, R. (2010). *The online learning imperative: A solution to three looming crises in education* [Issue brief]. Washington, DC: Alliance for Excellent Education.

Xu, Z., Hannaway, J., & Taylor, C. (2008). *Making a difference? The effects of Teach For America in high school.* Washington DC: The Urban Institute and CALDER. Retrieved on March 13, 2008 from http://www.urban.org/UploadedPDF/411642_Teach_America.pdf

Index

CORWIN

A SAGE Company

The Corwin logo—a raven striding across an open book—represents the union of courage and learning. Corwin is committed to improving education for all learners by publishing books and other professional development resources for those serving the field of PreK–12 education. By providing practical, hands-on materials, Corwin continues to carry out the promise of its motto: **"Helping Educators Do Their Work Better."**